BATTLEBAGS

BRITISH AIRSHIPS OF THE FIRST WORLD WAR

BATTLEBAGS

BRITISH AIRSHIPS OF THE FIRST WORLD WAR
An Illustrated History

CES MOWTHORPE

WRENS PARK

A Sutton Publishing Book

This edition published in 1998 by Wrens Park Publishing, an im print of
W.J. Williams & Son Ltd

This book was designed and produced by
Alan Sutton Publishing Limited, an imprint of Sutton Publishing Limited
Phoenix Mill · Far Thrupp · Stroud · Gloucestershire

British Library Cataloguing in Publication Data

A catalogue record for this book is available from the British Library.

ISBN 0905 778 138

Typeset in 10/13 Sabon.
Typesetting and origination by
Sutton Publishing Limited.
Printed in Great Britain by
WBC Limited, Bridgend, Mid-Glam organ.

Dedicated to the late David Cook of Tynemouth, Northumberland,
son of Flying Officer George Cook, Cardington Tower Officer,
and ex-airship coxswain.
At the time of his death,
David Cook's knowledge of British airships
was unsurpassed.

CONTENTS

ILLUSTRATIONS

PREFACE

An avid aviation enthusiast, and practising pilot since the age of sixteen, the study of airships has been a major interest of mine for forty years. I was born in the era of R.101 – R.100 was built just 'down the road at Howden' – and my parents frequently retold stories about wartime 'Zepps' – 'petrol tanks thrown overboard after the Zeppelin was damaged by the Atwick gun' – Howden 'Pigs', and Lowthorpe mooring out station. These, and other stories, stimulated in me a great curiosity about this, now, bygone form of flying.

During the late 1940s and 1950s, reliable sources of information about airships were few. Because of the huge advances in aeroplanes made during the Second World War, as far as Europe was concerned, airships had become as extinct as the dinosaur. The excellent Zeppelin Museum on the shores of Lake Constance at Friedrichshafen, Germany, had been wiped out by RAF bombing raids.

In Britain a wealth of information was hidden away, or lost, during the Second World War, and research has required seemingly endless time and money. Local records were non-existent because of security measures in force during the First World War. Even known deaths were not recorded in the usual 'civilian' manner. Then, in the early 1960s, I wrote a brief account for *Yorkshire Air News* of a 'Coastal' airship, C.11, from Howden that had hit a hill at Scarborough in April 1917. This opened a wide door. A Mr David Cook from Tynemouth (see the dedication) read the article and arranged to visit me. A friendship formed, and through

his late father's connections with airships, a considerable source of material emerged. Knowing I had a serious ambition to write what we called 'a comprehensive book' about British airships, David passed on much valuable information prior to his untimely death.

David Cook's father was F/O George Cook, Tower Officer in charge of the mooring mast at Cardington, in Bedfordshire. His service had started at Farnborough, with the then Naval Wing of No. 1 Company, Air Battalion. As coxswain he flew in *Beta, Delta*, several 'Coastals', Nos. 4, 5 and 6 at Howden (as part of the Rigid Trials Crew), No. 9r, No. 23r and finally R.31. It was on the latter that he was responsible, with six volunteers, for securing the upper fin when this collapsed in mid-air. Some days later, while clambering high inside R.31 examining the gas-cells, he was overcome by leaking hydrogen and fell unconscious into the keel, suffering serious injuries.

David's work took him around the country and he utilised this to visit as many of his late father's ex-airship friends as possible. Knowing my wish to write this book he freely allowed me to take notes and copy any of his photographs. His great interest in the Royal Navy's 'lighter-than-air' craft led him to mount a number of exhibitions of airship photographs around the North of England and to broadcast on local radio.

Over the last twenty years a number of excellent books about airships have been written (see the Bibliography) but they only cover the subject generally. No previous publication has attempted to identify and describe operations of each single airship. Having attempted to do this, I can appreciate why! This book has taken thirty years to complete – not the writing, the research. Without David Cook's assistance my task would have been infinitely more difficult and many of the better photographs perhaps never published.

Another great help was the late Wg Cdr 'Wally' Dunn OBE. An ex-Halton 'brat', as wireless operator he flew out of Howden on 'North Seas' during 1920–21. Posted to fly on R.38 to America he was bitterly disappointed when this was cancelled and he was sent to Gibraltar on flying-boats instead. Listening out from Gibraltar he was 'working' his chum on R.38 when 'transmissions ceased abruptly!' R.38 had broken up in flight over the Humber! During the Second World War, Wg Cdr Dunn was Signals Officer to No. 617 Squadron (the Dambusters) and the man who handed the famous 'Nigger' message to Barnes-Wallis. He had a wealth of airship knowledge which he freely shared.

ACKNOWLEDGEMENTS

I would like to pay thanks Mr David Cook, son of the late Sqn Ldr George Cook, Tower Officer at Cardington, for his assistance with this book, and also to the late Wg Cdr 'Wally' Dunn OBE, of Bridlington, East Yorkshire. I have outlined their assistance more fully in the Preface to this book

Their contributions made this book possible. Of equal importance are their 'old pals' who passed on so many valuable contributions which have ended up in these pages. Their names are forever linked with the lighter-than-air pioneers of this country: Beckford-Ball, 'Jerry' Long, Havers, York-Moore and many others. Wg Cdr Dunn's association with Sir Barnes Wallis (from their Dambusters work in No. 617 Sqn) proved very helpful. Tim Elmhirst, nephew of the late AVM T.W. Elmhirst, was also instrumental, lending me a copy of his late uncle's *Memoirs*. Countless other ex-airshipmen have unwittingly contributed information through their contact with the above people – which eventually found its way into my records. If any of these, or their relatives, get in touch with me I will be delighted to acknowledge them if further editions are published.

Thanks must also go to Mr Naylor of the Royal Aeronautical Society; Mr Graeme Mottram and Mr Richardson of the Fleet Air Arm Museum, Yeovilton; countless members of the Public Record Office at Kew, who have rendered me vital assistance during my researches there; and Nick Forder, compiler of 'Bookshelf' in *Cross & Cockade* – the assistance rendered to me by members of *Cross & Cockade*, the Society of World War One Aero Historians, has been invaluable. I must also thank a kindred spirit, Brian Turpin, whose knowledge of airship development in general and British airships in particular, is among the foremost in Britain today; he spent much time reading my proofs and offering corrections and improvements. The details of the Vickers Japanese 'Parseval' had eluded my research efforts but Brian was able to remedy this, as well as providing a number of photographs. Philip and Margaret Neaverson of the Airship Heritage Trust photographic archives, Cardington, went to great lengths to oblige with two rare photographs. The Airship Heritage Trust's (previously FOCAS) magazine *Dirigible* has contributed some interesting details. Thanks also to Tom Jameson, of Hull, for his assistance with Appendix D, RNAS Howden.

One of the most important contributors has been Stuart Leslie from Scarborough. The photographic collection JMB/GSL and his tremendous knowledge of the early years of the RNAS/RFC/RAF have been placed at my disposal at all times. Thank you again Stuart.

And lastly, but not least, to my son-in-law Michael Walters of Walters Office World, Peterborough, go my personal thanks for unlimited use of his photocopier and paper – not to mention my temporary disruption of his business.

INTRODUCTION

When the average person thinks of airships, they think immediately of the huge Zeppelin-type rigid craft. The Zeppelins' excellent performance quite rightly made them a household name, which became synonymous with all rigid airships, whether or not they were Zeppelins. By the same token, whenever British airships are mentioned, people think first of the R.101 disaster! This implies that only the Germans knew how to build airships. Certainly, German expertise with large rigids was unchallenged. But how many people know that the Royal Navy had operated a fleet of at least 211 airships during the First World War?

Airships were the logical development of the balloon. Balloons were simply large bags, called envelopes, filled with a lighter-than-air gas that literally floated through the air. They could gain or lose height by discharging small quantities of ballast or gas.

Successful balloon flights had been made for over a century, but only at the whim of the prevailing wind. The invention of the petrol-engine provided a way of escaping this dependence on the wind. By giving the envelope a streamlined profile, powered balloons could be guided through the air in a similar manner to ships crossing the seas – hence their name 'airships'.

At the turn of the twentieth century, quite a number of small non-rigid airships had flown successfully on the Continent, and Count Zeppelin in Germany was building the first of more than a hundred giant rigid ones. Until this time Great Britain had been accessible only by sea, but events in 1909 and 1910 changed this situation. In July 1909 an aeroplane flown by Bleriot crossed the English Channel. Then, in 1910, four more cross-Channel flights were made – and three of these were by airships.

That this should be the case is not really surprising. Firstly, the duration of an aeroplane flight was measured in minutes, whereas airship flights were all of several hours duration. Thus while Bleriot had struggled to make it across the Channel, a Clement-Bayard airship was able to fly direct from Paris to Wormwood Scrubs.

Secondly, while an aeroplane carried only its pilot, airships could carry at least two, without difficulty: the Clement-Bayard mentioned above had in fact carried seven people on its flight to Wormwood Scrubs. This established the early supremacy of airships over heavier-than-air machines in terms of payload or carrying capacity.

Another important factor was that an airship did not have to descend if its engine failed. It could became a free-floating balloon, allowing the engine to be repaired in flight, or, at worst, a relatively safe landing could be made by slowly valving (releasing) gas. It also followed that the airship's weight-lifting capability enabled two engines to be carried, which further enhanced both reliability and performance.

Although at first it seemed a simple task to suspend a car containing engine and crew below a streamlined elongated gas-bag, it soon became apparent that the task was not that simple. For example, if the gas-bag was too long and thin, it sagged in the middle.

Therefore one reduced the length and increased the width – thus creating more drag, which required a larger (and heavier!) engine. This in turn called for a bigger envelope – and so on. This relationship between length and width is known as the 'fineness ratio'.

Thus the aim of all airship designers was to produce a large envelope and attach to it a suitable car containing crew, payload and engine or engines. But the further below the envelope they were attached, the greater the drag. The greater the drag, the more the power required to control its direction! A common sight was even the most powerful airships 'crabbing' sideways in a strong crosswind due to their great side-area.

TYPES OF AIRSHIP

There were three basic types of airship. First was the simple non-rigid. This was a gas-bag, the shape of which was determined by the internal pressure, with internal ballonets of air collected from the slipstream, assisting in its control.

The second type was the rigid airship. This was the Zeppelin solution, a strong but light outer framework, consisting of radial frames joined together with longitudinals, covered in linen. This framework contained a gas-bag between each radial frame. The beautiful R.100 had fifteen gas-bags and a fineness ratio of five-and-a-half to one. The third type, a cross between the other two types, was the semi-rigid. These had envelopes which retained their shape through the internal pressure of the gas they contained, but they also had a keel running along the bottom, giving greater rigidity than a simple envelope.

After a fitful start, the method of 'steering' airships settled down to a more or less common system of cruciform (cross-shaped) surfaces at the rear of the envelope. To these were attached rudders and elevators.

Swivelling propellers were popular in pre-1915 ships but were soon discarded because of their extra weight (though they have seen a revival in the 1980s due to modern developments in materials). All airships carried a considerable amount of ballast they could release to compensate for the loss of gas.

The greater the volume of gas that an airship contained, the more weight – in the form of engines, fuel and payload – it could lift. In the early days the German Zeppelin, which used light but inflammable hydrogen gas, appeared to be the ideal. Even with multiple engines and several tons of fuel, a Zeppelin had a payload of several tons. Multiple engines were necessary if regular flights of hundreds of miles were to become the norm: they ensured control and airspeed could be maintained if one (or more) had to be shut down for any length of time.

The design of rigids started with two engines, increasing rapidly until the final wartime Zeppelin 'L.70' class had seven 245 hp Maybachs. By 1915, these rigids could leave their bases on the Continent and navigate – with no external aids – over most of England, carrying a bomb load of several tons. Unless exceptional bad weather or a lucky interception by Britain's defences intervened, a return to base was certain. No other type of aircraft attained this standard for many years.

At the other end of the scale, the Royal Navy's non-rigids too were capable of flight quite beyond that of their aeroplane equivalents. Their natural ability to fly 'low and slow', or remain stationary if required, were excellent characteristics. They were ideal for escorting shipping and searching the surface of the sea for a submarine's periscope or a floating mine. They could also be built quickly and manned by easily-trained volunteer crews.

However, it must be appreciated that, except for two tragic occasions, the Royal

Navy's 'battle-bags' operated in airspace over which Germany had no control. On both occasions when German fighter planes were encountered – near the North Hinder Light vessel, by 'Coastals' C.17 and C.27 – the airships were immediately shot down with the loss of their crews. It was not until nearly 1917 that the Zeppelin – which was always in a potentially hostile environment when over England – could be caught by aeroplanes. Even then, if handled expertly and dropping tons of ballast, it had every chance of outclimbing any intercepting aircraft.

Despite the tremendous advances made by aeroplanes, it was not until the Second World War that they overtook the airship in terms of range and carrying capacity. Even in 1938–39, when Germany was investigating the tall RDF/Radar towers that had appeared around the eastern and southern coasts of Britain, the only aircraft with the range and duration to carry the radio equipment necessary was the Zeppelin LZ.130 (*Graf Zeppelin 2*) which flew off the coastline on two separate occasions, for several days.

The reasoning behind the use of the Royal Navy's non-rigid airships was this. A U-boat would sight an airship long before the airship could possibly sight the U-boat. Hence the U-boat would be forced to submerge, and thus limited to a speed of, at best, only 6 or 7 knots. Therefore, with an airship overhead, shipping could outpace the U-boats. To get into an attacking position, the U-boats would need to be ahead of their targets. Submerged, this was not often practical. Furthermore, should a U-boat surface, or fire a torpedo while an airship was in the vicinity, a radio call to the nearest surface craft brought immediate assistance.

By late 1917 developments in echo-location (ASDIC) and depth-charges meant a detected U-boat faced almost certain destruction. Indeed, the proud boast of the Royal Naval Airship Service was that no ship was lost if airships were overhead. (To be scrupulously accurate, this was not correct. On Boxing Day 1917 two ships were torpedoed while forming up a convoy off Falmouth, under the escort of 'Coastals' from Mullion. But it was still a worthwhile boast!)

Vital to the building of non-rigid airships was the production of the envelopes. Messrs Vickers quickly cornered the market by forming a subsidiary, the Ioco Rubber & Waterproofing Company, later Ioco Ltd. The company also subcontracted to the 'Macintosh trade'. The envelopes were made of two thicknesses of rubberised fabric with rubber between and on the inside surface. The envelopes were doped (weatherproofed) on the outside, eventually using an aluminium dope.

Ballonets for the later rigids were also produced by Ioco, which took over the 'Palace' ballroom at Douglas, Isle of Man, where the huge ballonets were inflated with compressed air, to test for leaks.

The semi-rigid airship never found favour in this country, although several of the early airships built or flown at Farnborough were of this type. The discovery of the 'Eta' patch (see p. 12) rendered them unnecessary. Italy, however, spawned many successful semi-rigids. Its 'V', 'P' and 'M' classes were much larger than most non-rigid ships, but proved to be efficient in the Mediterranean theatre during the First World War, no doubt helped by the relatively calmer Mediterranean conditions. They carried out many bombing raids. Britain bought one of these 'M' ships (and flew it back to Kingsnorth, but it was too late to take an active part in war in the North Sea.

A BRIEF HISTORY

Before looking at the various airships, it is useful to present a brief summary of the

Royal Navy's involvement with airships, and their operation. This involvement went back to January 1914, when the newly formed Royal Naval Air Service (RNAS) took over the Army's existing fleet of small non-rigids. Before that, the Royal Engineers had pioneered this branch of the service with considerable success at Farnborough, the then home of British Service flying. Fortunately most of the Army's flying personnel were re-mustered into the RNAS, thus establishing a core of expertise.

In 1909 the Admiralty had ordered and subsequently built a Zeppelin-type rigid airship. Naval Rigid Airship No. 1 – or 'Mayfly', to give it its unofficial name – was constructed at Barrow by Messrs Vickers. On 24 September 1911, while being brought out of her shed, the 'Mayfly' broke her back when caught by a sudden gust of wind. She was broken up in situ, the Admiralty then washing its hands of large rigid airships!

However, the German Zeppelin was proving so efficient that Vickers was given another order for a rigid in 1913, although it was not confirmed until March 1914. This was No. 9r, based largely upon drawings and photographs taken by the French when the German Army's Zeppelin Z.IV had made an emergency landing at Luneville in April 1913. Due to various delays, No. 9r did not fly until late 1916.

At the outbreak of the First World War, the newly formed RNAS had just seven non-rigid airships, with only two, No. 3 and No. 4 (see Apppendix A), fit for operational use. Three Astra-Torres airships were on order from France, but on the other hand the construction of three German Parsevals was naturally cancelled. Within the first few weeks of war, the loss of the cruisers HMS *Aboukir*, HMS *Hogue* and HMS *Cressey* to a single U-boat, plus the torpedoing of the battleship HMS *Formidable* by U.24 during the first few hours of 1915, forced the Admiralty to muster all resources against the submarine menace. One of the options was to provide air cover, that, with the use of wireless telegraphy (W/T), could call up surface craft such as destroyers to deal with any U-boats that were sighted.

On 28 February 1915 the Admiralty issued a specification for a new class of airship. Briefly, the specification required the rapid development of a small airship with a maximum speed of 50 m.p.h., a duration of 8 hours, carrying a crew of two and 160 lb of bombs plus a W/T set and 'capable of being flown by young midshipmen with small-boat training'.

Experimental work on the RNAS's airships had moved from Farnborough to the new RNAS station at Kingsnorth. There, under the CO, Wg Cdr N.F. Usborne, together with Flt Lt Cave-Browne-Cave and F.M. Green of the Royal Aircraft Factory at Farnborough, this urgent requirement for small airships was quickly put in hand. The story of these small airships, which became known as the 'SS' class, is told fully under the appropriate section of this book. This was the real start of the British airship programme which, under the care of the Royal Navy, expanded rapidly. Even though the Navy invested heavily in its heavier-than-air (aeroplane) branch throughout the First World War, the airship remained specially suitable for maritime duties.

Initially the 'SS' ships were based at 'war stations' around the Channel and Irish Sea. Their somewhat limited performance, coupled with relatively inexperienced crews, required close proximity to the sea. When the larger 'Coastal' airships became available operationally, the need for coastal stations was less acute and a chain of large war stations, suitable for the proposed large rigids, was built adjacent to the East Coast at Pulham, Howden, East Fortune and Longside. The training station at Cranwell was added later.

With the coming of the 'Zeros' came the mooring out sites. These were based upon the pre-war experience of mooring airships in the open air, sheltered by trees, in quarries, etc. Although there was no accommodation for crews and ground staff, except in tents, and all the major servicing had to be done at the nearest war station, these mooring out sites cut down the time wasted flying cross-country to the coast. By 1918 there were quite a number, usually in small woods. Sometimes pits were dug for the airship cars, which made for easier handling.

During 1915, flights of 6 to 8 hours were rare, the average being under 4 hours. As the 'Coastals' got into their operational stride, 12 hour flights became possible, but infrequent. Once the 'Zero' and 'Coastal Star' classes became operational in 1917, 12 hour flights became quite common. Consider the discomfort of these pioneer flyers, sitting cramped and exposed to the cold, for up to 12 hours at a time, being 'humped, bumped and buggered around' in turbulence, after crossing the coastline on their last few miles back to their base. Any head-wind at all reduced their ground speed, sometimes to as low as 5–10 m.p.h.!

Despite the limited capabilities of the early airships, in 1914 No. 3 operated briefly from Dunkirk, and later on SS–40 made short forays over the front line. 'SS' ships also operated in the Eastern Mediterranean out of Imbros and Mudros (as No. 1 Airship Expeditionary Force), though with relatively little success, mainly due to the heat which both depleted the 'useful lift' and reduced engine performance. RNAS Marquise, an airfield on the French side of the Channel, operated a few airships in conjunction with RNAS Capel up to late 1915, when the French took over Marquise.

As a result of operational experience – and trial and error – during the early days, many modifications were made to the airships. It will be noted that early 'SSs' had four tail surfaces, two horizontal (with dihedral) and fitted with elevators, plus two 'vertical', also fitted with rudders, at approximately 45 degrees, below the tail. This was calculated the best format for good directional control, which was always a problem with airships. Practice however proved that the same control could be obtained by fitting a single vertical fin and rudder, thus reducing drag. Eventually most 'SSs' were thus modified and, indeed, it became standard for all airships. As the envelope capacity increased on 'SSs', 'Zeros' and similar, from 60,000 to 70,000 and in some cases 100,000 cu ft, it became the practice to fit an extra fin (without a rudder) immediately forward of and attached to the original. Fuel tanks, originally fitted 'somewhere' on the car, were eventually slung mid-way up the envelope in canvas slings, feeding the engines by gravity. As the small airships made longer flights, more tanks were slung on each side. Sometimes the later ships carried six, three each side.

Calculating how many airships the Royal Navy flew during the First World War has proved a difficult task. One reliable figure from Admiralty records shows 103 airships on strength at the Armistice in November 1918. This does not take into account ships lost or taken out of service during hostilities. Altogether a total of 226 airships of all classes, constructed and reconstructed, is given. However, this number is almost certainly an underestimate, for several reasons. For example, the initial batch of 'SS' ships was ordered 'with 100 per cent spares'! Also, by 1916 new envelopes for all classes were being made on a steady production basis. Therefore it is quite probable that a number of hybrid ships were rigged on stations for training purposes: the record shows that at Howden in August 1918, 'an American crew, assisted by British crews, created a new "SSZ" class non-rigid from a spare envelope and spare car'. If it had not caught fire while the radio was being tested, and destroyed all the ships in the Howden shed (including new rigid R.27), its existence would never have come to light!

OPERATIONS

As with all British aircrew, the 'sailors' who flew Royal Naval airships were volunteers. Initially the RNAS took over the experienced airshipmen at Farnborough, including some civilians such as F.M. Green, a senior technician. Then, as requirements grew, volunteers were brought in from the Royal Navy. By the end of 1915 a direct entry was established for airship crews who went straight onto flying training after completing their Part One (Initial) training. Naturally the majority of wartime crews were Royal Navy Volunteer Reserve (RNVR) but a few regular RN officers volunteered throughout hostilities. All captains of wartime airships were officers, while W/T and engineering crew were usually ratings.

Right from earliest days, pioneers such as Cunningham, Usborne, Sueter and Masterman developed the lighter-than-air branch of the RN. Unlike their wartime contemporaries, the RNVR, these hard-core professionals were not particularly lovers of flying. They simply saw the airship as a weapon to be developed against the enemy, and develop it they did!

Beyond any doubt, the greatest single factor common to the British non-rigid airships was the 'Eta' patch. Developed during 1912 by the Farnborough team, it was first used on the 1913 airship *Eta*. Prior to this development, the suspension of any car or gondola was from some form of bridle, which formed the base of the 'net' containing the envelope, much like on a normal balloon. As the airships became bigger, this 'net and

bridle' system became difficult to apply – hence the 'long' cars of the early non-rigids. The invention of the 'Eta' patch meant that anything could be attached directly to the envelope, subject to weight and aerodynamic forces. Though the trefoil envelopes of the 'Coastal' and 'North Sea' class airships had a different suspension system, based on internal 'curtains', their tail surfaces, etc, used the 'Eta' patch (or similar) for support. It was this development that enabled the Kingsnorth team to attach an aeroplane fuselage to a gas-bag, thereby creating an airship!

While Kingsnorth dealt with experimental matters, it was on the war stations that air and ground crews slowly but surely mastered the thousand-and-one everyday problems that arose. For example, the first 'SS' ships were plagued with overheating of their Renault engines. Designed for aeroplanes, which required high power for (relatively) short periods, the engines were cooled by a 50–60 m.p.h. airflow through their radiators. Fitted to airships, which in 1915 seldom flew at more than 30 m.p.h., and often for 2 or 3 hours, they overheated and would seize up if not stopped. During these early days, many engineers became adept at restarting the engine, after it had cooled down, by balancing on a skid, several hundred feet in the air, and flicking the propeller over! Gradually, with the introduction of larger radiators and improved engine-handling, crews were managing regular 4 or 5 hour flights in these same machines by mid-1917.

When the first 'SS' class ships became operational in 1915, they seldom flew in windspeeds greater than 15 m.p.h., due to the difficulty of handling them, particularly on the ground. Eventually, with practice, the handling crews attained much more expertise and by 1917 an airship station was able to operate in windspeeds of 30–35 m.p.h., which meant monthly flying hours rose sharply.

Another major problem was caused by magnetos. Prior to the outbreak of war, all magnetos for British engines (automobile, marine or aircraft) were made by the German firm Bosch, a supply that was cut off with the outbreak of hostilities. Although a stock was in hand, Britain had to start manufacturing its own. This took some time and unfortunately many of these British magnetos proved faulty when in service.

No-one will ever know the cost of these faulty magnetos in terms of men and machines lost. Take, for example, 'Coastal' airship C.16. In August 1916, C.16 made her maiden flight from Kingsnorth to East Fortune. On 28 August she set out on her first 'war-patrol'. After an hour, one engine failed through a faulty magneto. Within the next hour the other engine failed of the same cause! Luckily an onshore wind blew C.16 into Coldingham Bay, near Berwick, where her captain 'ripped' (deflated) the envelope. Thankfully the crew was saved, but C.16 was a complete wreck. How many times had this occurred with aeroplanes on the Western Front, with no survivors, before British-made magnetos reached an acceptable reliability by the end of the war?

However, if they suffered an unrepairable engine failure, these small airships often drifted many miles off course until land appeared: at least one airship based on Anglesey drifted across the Irish Sea and came down in Ireland. Sometimes a passing ship would manage to grab the trail ropes or grapnel and tow the airship to safety. When non-rigid airships lost power, their air ballonets lost pressure, and so the non-rigids frequently assumed some peculiar shapes!

Of course, one solution to the problem was for the ship to carry spare magnetos. The following narrative, from Air Marshal 'Tommy' Elmhirst's *Recollections* is pertinent:

'Airship engines were not wholly reliable in 1917, luckily in light winds we could maintain height and position on patrol with one engine, while the other was under repair. I had an imperturbable "crew" engineer. I can see him now sitting on the engine bearers with his legs dangling in space disconnecting two faulty magnetos and fitting and timing new ones.'

Another of Air Marshal Elmhirst's anecdotes tells of his engineer, Scott, who was later to form part of R.34's crew on her trans-Atlantic flight. Scott, having had to close down the aft engine of his 'Coastal' because of violent vibrations, crawled along the car's handrail – the normal method of communicating – and reported that the tip of one propeller blade was missing! Unperturbed, he waited for the engine to cool, then sat on it and shaped both blades with a saw and file until they matched. Upon restarting the engine, it ran smoothly and got the 'Coastal' home.

When bombs were dropped into the sea during attacks on U-boats, for example, or sea-mines exploded by the airship's Lewis-gun, it was common practice, once the emergency was over, to hover low above the surface and trail a canvas bucket. Full of stunned fish, the bucket was hoisted until it was suspended just below the car for the flight back to base thus ensuring a regular supply of fresh fish for the messes.

TRAINING

Training of airship pilots soon got under way in typical Naval fashion. After an initial general training – usually two months, as with the seaman branch – the PFO (Probationary Flying Officer) reported to Wormwood Scrubs for 'Balloon Training'. This consisted of about a dozen flights in one of 'The Scrubs' balloons. These training balloons all had girls names, such as *Joan*, *Alice*, *May*, and *Hazel*. Most had baskets which carried up to five trainees and an instructor. About 10 hours flying, including a night flight, took place, and then the trainee, subject to reaching the required standard, went solo in a smaller two-man craft. Among the instructors at Wormwood Scrubs in 1917 were a Lt Vickers, a Mr Parkhurst and Dr Barton, the builder of the Barton airship. Until Cranwell became operational as a training station, pilots – now commissioned as flight sub-lieutenants – then proceeded to their war stations where they passed out as pilots on 'SS' ships.

Airship crews did not consider their task particularly dangerous, despite flying with hot exhausts only a few feet below thousands of cubic feet of inflammable hydrogen! Excellent handling practices were the order of the day. Although they were seated in an open car, unable to move for up to 8 hours, blasted by the slipstream and often in sub-zero temperatures, their keenness rarely waned. On numerous occasions airships would land and the crew, frozen stiff with cold, had to be carried bodily from their positions by ground personnel. Bear in mind that at the Armistice, in 1918, a number of 'Zero' and 'SS-Twin' flights had exceeded 24 hours! Nonetheless, airshipmen felt their lot was infinitely better than the 'poor bloody infantry' in the trenches or the aeroplane pilots who flew over the lines.

Air Marshal Elmhirst has this to say about his days as captain of C.19:

'Weather and serviceability permitting, C.19 was seldom off patrol. Dispatched at dawn and told to stay on patrol for at least 12 hours was hard going. Hard on the eyes, watching the gas-bag pressure, watching the course the coxswain was steering, and one eye all the time looking for the enemy whom I never saw. He could see me from 20 miles distant and submerge. I could only hope to catch sight of a periscope 400 yards away. It was hard on the hands and I came home with blisters from the elevator control wheel after a "bumpy" day, also hard on the backside sitting concentrated for long hours. Food was a pleasant relief and a problem. It did not always taste well in the slipstream of an open-exhaust engine using castor oil! I eventually settled for a large packet of marmalade sandwiches and a bottle of Malvern water. My crew and I did not smoke or "drink" in the air but just looked forward to a cigarette and a beer on landing.'

At first the Royal Navy discounted the rigid airship, concentrating upon the larger non-rigids such as No. 3 and No. 4. However, after the Battle of Jutland in May 1916 – where it was erroneously assumed that Zeppelins had warned the Germans of the disposition of the British Grand Fleet – they rapidly changed their minds. Admiral Beatty on one occasion stated that for scouting purposes 'one "Zeppelin" was worth three cruisers'! The rush was then on to build British rigid airships. As a stop-gap and to gain experience in co-operating with scouting airships, the Grand Fleet hoped the 'North Sea' class would suffice.

Despite teething trouble, some good work was accomplished between the Fleet and the 'Coastal' class until the first rigids became operational in late 1917. Despite operating ships many years behind the Zeppelin in design, and being forced to adapt very quickly, the rigids' crews were not found wanting. Taken from experienced 'Coastal' men, these pioneers were assembled as Rigid Trial Crews at Howden in 1917, under Cdr Masterman, and exercised on Parsevals Nos. 4, 5 and 6. When Vickers' No. 9r finally arrived, there were abundant trained crewmen available to man the newer ships like this now coming into service.

EARLY AIRSHIPS

From the foregoing it would appear that all British airships were in some way attached to the Services. Admittedly, the bulk of airship operations occurred during the First World War and shortly afterwards. Civilian airmen, however, had played an important part in the early days. It was Stanley Spencer, whose Spencer Brothers company manufactured balloon envelopes, who in 1903 had fitted an engine to an elongated envelope and made the first navigable flight in this country. Brazilian Alberto Santos-Dumont had flown similar airships in Paris since 1898, and as the Spencer Brothers were involved in the ballooning scene it is possible that, to some extent, they based their design on Santos-Dumont's craft. However, this in no way detracts from Stanley Spencer's achievement.

Another pioneer was Dr Barton of London. He constructed a semi-rigid airship which actually took to the air on 22 July 1905. As this airship broke its back on this flight, its performance was never recorded. However, Dr Barton crops up regularly as a pilot in the pre-war ballooning events. In early 1915 his services were snapped up by the RNAS and he trained many future airship pilots in 'free ballooning' at Wormwood Scrubs, prior to their further training in powered airships.

Perhaps the most under-rated pioneer was E.T. Willows. With no previous experience, he constructed six small airships between 1905 and 1915. They made several notable flights and one was sold to the Admiralty. Had the First World War not broken out, and with more investment in his enterprise, the name of Willows could have become world famous. However, his strong belief in swivelling propellers – which were complicated and expensive to produce – put

him out of the running when the RNAS required small airships quickly and cheaply.

Whenever British airships are mentioned, Vickers of Barrow-in-Furness must come to the fore. A private firm, heavily involved with the manufacture of submarines and armaments for the Royal Navy, it was a natural choice for the construction of airships. However, as the First World War progressed, the Royal Navy felt that Messrs Vickers were tending to dictate terms. Therefore Messrs Shorts were brought in to build the two wooden ships R.31 and R.32, while Messrs Armstrong at Barlow, Yorkshire, and Messrs Beardmore at Inchinnan, Scotland, acted virtually as sub-contractors to Vickers for the '23' class rigids. In addition, the Admiralty employed them directly for the '33' class and beyond.

Prior to the war, Vickers had negotiated with the German Parseval firm for rights to build their large non-rigids. After the outbreak of war, Vickers proceeded to build the P.5, P.6 and P.7, basically to the original German designs. This encouraged Vickers to set up an envelope-manufacturing plant which cornered the market for envelopes and gas-bags.

When hostilities ended, Vickers was the second largest rigid airship builder in the world, surpassed only by the Zeppelin concern in Germany. Its design team under Barnes-Wallis was the equal of any competitor: Barnes-Wallis's R.80 – though small, because of the size of shed available – was years ahead of anything except the latest Zeppelins. Naturally, when it was decided to build two large rigids in the mid-1920s, one by the Government, the other by a private firm, the Vickers proposal was chosen. As we shall see in the last chapter, these two rigids were to become the 'ultimate' British airships – R.100 and R.101.

AIRSHIP STATIONS
1914 TO 1918

RNAS AIRSHIP STATIONS (SHOWN ○)

1. Longside (Angus)
3. East Fortune (East Lothian)
7. Howden (Yorks.)
8. Cranwell (Lincs.)
9. Pulham (Norfolk)
10. Kingsnorth (Kent)
13. Capel (Kent)
14. Polegate (Sussex)
19. Mullion (Cornwall)
21. Pembroke (Pembrokeshire)
22. Anglesey (Anglesey)
24. Luce Bay (Wigtownshire)

RNAS AIRSHIP SUB-STATIONS/MOORING-OUT SITES (SHOWN ●)

2. Auldbar (Angus)
4. Chathill (Northumberland)
5. Kirkleatham (Yorks.)
6. Lowthorpe (Yorks.)
11. Godmersham Park (Kent)
12. West Mersham (Kent)
15. Slindon (Sussex)
16. Upton (Dorset)
17. Bridport (Dorset)
18. Laira (Devon)
20. Bude (Cornwall)
23. Ramsey (Isle of Man)
25. Ballyliffan (Donegal)
26. Larne (Antrim)
27. Malahide (Co. Dublin)
28. Killeagh (Co. Cork)

CHAPTER 1

BRITAIN'S EARLY AIRSHIPS

Rapid wartime expansion of the RNAS's lighter-than-air branch was possible only because of the expertise which had come from the Army airship pioneers at Farnborough. By the time the Royal Navy took over in January 1914, the non-rigid airship was a practical reality. It is therefore essential to briefly examine what airships had flown, in Britain, prior to the outbreak of hostilities in August 1914.

The original pioneers, including civilians, had overcome tremendous difficulties in order to navigate the skies. The first successful navigable aircraft flown in Britain was a small airship. Built by Stanley Spencer, a balloon-maker and aeronaut, it was 75 ft long, with a diameter of 20 ft and capacity of approximately 20,000 cu ft. Its 3 hp water-cooled Sims engine drove a 10 ft diameter propeller at 250 revolutions per minute.

In 1902, with Stanley Spencer piloting from its small platform, it took off from the grounds of Crystal Palace. Flying an erratic course, it landed safely at Eastcote 100 minutes later. A number of further flights took place at both Crystal Palace and Ranelagh Gardens.

Spencer's small craft was modified over a period of years, with a new envelope, a redesigned car and a more powerful engine. Now capable of carrying a crew of two, it made many successful flights up to 1908.

Stanley Spencer never failed to use his ship's envelope for some kind of advertisement, no doubt earning some revenue! In 1913 Bovril, the meat extract company, ordered a small airship from Messrs Spencer & Co. Of 40,000 cu ft capacity and 96 ft long, it was powered by a 40 hp Green engine. It is possible that this airship was constructed from parts of the previous Spencer airships, although the two chain-driven propellers on the Bovril ship were on out-riggers, port and starboard.

The envelope carried the slogan, in large letters, 'Give Him Bovril', and August and September 1913 saw the airship making many flights around London, including displays at Hendon, with 'an attacking aeroplane'! On one occasion a flight above 4,000 ft was made. On another, the airship was kept on the ground for several days following a forced landing at Sunderland Farm, Biggleswade, where the car and envelope were separated to prevent damage. Eventually gas was brought from London and the craft was re-rigged. Carrying a crew of two (the pilot being a Mr Bagnall), it took off, then landed at Sutton in Cambridgeshire before flying back to base.

Another pioneer was Dr F.A. Barton, who in 1903 received an award of £4,000 after demonstrating a clockwork model airship to the War Office. Building a shed in North London, near Alexandra Palace, he proceeded to construct a semi-rigid airship, 180 ft long, with 230,000 cu ft capacity and two 50 hp engines. The maiden flight, with himself and a crew of four, took place on 22 July 1905. Sadly, after a successful launch, engine problems caused the ship to be swept downwind, out of control. A safe landing was made, but the airship was a total loss after folding up during the final stages of the landing.

Meanwhile, Splott, on the southern side of Cardiff, had been the scene of intense activity.

A Stanley Spencer airship taking off from Crystal Palace, 22 September 1902. (Nick Forder)

The Spencer 'Bovril' airship, 1913. (Messrs 'Bovril' via the Airship Heritage Trust)

The Barton airship on its only flight, 22 July 1905. The flight ended in an uncontrolled landing. (Fleet Air Arm Museum; neg. no. A/SHIP/369)

A modified Spencer airship, *c.* 1908. (The Science Museum; neg. no. 2020/78)

During 1904, E.T. Willows, with the financial backing of his father and a Capt William Beadle – whose own airship had failed to fly at Alexandra Palace, London on 3 November 1903 – was building a 72 ft long, 18 ft diameter airship of 12,000 cu ft capacity. This was known as the Willows No. 1. Powered by a 7 hp Peugeot motorcycle engine driving a 10 ft propeller at the stern, this craft incorporated Capt Beadle's system of two 'steering propellers' rotating at half the speed of the driving propeller. These steering propellers swivelled in the nose of a triangular keel which housed the engine and crew of two.

The maiden flight, of 85 minutes duration, took place on 5 September 1904, with No. 1 attaining a height of 120 ft. Further flights in 1904 included a demonstration to a Col J.E. Capper on behalf of the War Office.

Over the next two years several modifications were carried out, including lengthening the keel from 30 ft to 45 ft, and trying varying positions for the steering propellers. The result was an airship now known as the Willows No. 1A. Many flights took place, some in winds up to 10 m.p.h. Col Capper was 'keeping in touch' with progress, and he is credited with saying in 1908 that his own airship, the *Nulli Secundus*, 'Second to None', in fact 'came a bad second to the Willows 1A'.

Now operating on his own, with financial help from his father, Willows developed the steerable propellers a stage further. Taking out a patent (BP.14.434/1909) for swivelling propellers, one each side of the 'car', he built a second airship. Its varnished cotton envelope, streamlined, 86 ft long and with 21,000 cu ft capacity, was made by 'Spencer Bros Balloon Makers'. It had an internal ballonet in its base and was attached to a 58 ft boom from which hung the car, containing a 30 hp JAP air-cooled 8-cylinder engine, the pilot and a passenger. Between the boom and the envelope were a vertical fin and rudder for directional control. With swivelling propellers and this rudder, control was reported as excellent.

Known as the Willows No. 2, Willows' new airship made her maiden flight on 26 November 1909, and several extended flights took place over the next month. In 1910 Messrs Handley Page supplied Willows with a pair of new propellers 'of 200 lb thrust', and on 4 and 7 June of that year thousands of people massed to witness two flights in and out of the centre of Cardiff. On 6 August it made a flight across the Bristol Channel and on through the night to London, landing at Crystal Palace the next morning. From there, several more ascents were made, including one around St Paul's cathedral.

Around this time a new envelope of 32,000 cu ft capacity was ordered from the North British Rubber Co. Made in one of the galleries at Crystal Palace, it contained two ballonets, fore and aft, for trimming purposes. Attached to this envelope was No. 2's car, greatly strengthened and modified to carry an 'engineer', thus forming the Willows No. 3 airship, officially named *City of Cardiff*. She was inflated at Wormwood Scrubs and carried out her maiden flight on 29 October 1910.

At this time Willows employed as a mechanic a Mr Frank Gooden. On 4 November 1910, Willows and Gooden (who was to lose his life as a Farnborough test pilot during the First World War) made the first crossing of the English Channel by a British aircraft. Attempting to reach Paris, they had to force land at Corbehem, near Douai. The deflated airship was taken to the Clement-Bayard airship works at La Morte for repairs, before finally flying on to Issy-les-Moulineaux, Paris, where it landed on 7 January 1911. From there a number of passenger flights were carried out before *City of Cardiff* was transported back to Britain, by rail, on 11 January 1911. At this point Frank Gooden and Willows parted company.

For his achievements, Willows, a founder member of the Royal Aero Club, was selected to receive one of the first four Airship Pilot's Certificates on their first day of issue, which was 14 February 1911. Not only the youngest, he was also the only civilian to receive a certificate.

During the next month the Willows No. 3 was re-inflated and flown to Wolverhampton, where flights were offered to passengers at 3 guineas per 15 minutes or 5 guineas for a trip over the town.

Moving to a shed at Birmingham in 1912, Willows built his fourth airship, which had a 110 ft oiled-cotton, streamlined envelope of 24,000 cu ft capacity and two ballonets, with a maximum diameter of 18 ft 6 in. Attached to its long keel by steel struts was a torpedo-shaped car containing the pilot, passenger and engine, complete with swivelling propellers. Its original 24 hp air-cooled JAP engine was soon replaced by a 35 hp 3-cylinder Anzani. Cruciform tail surfaces with a vertical rudder were fitted at rear of the boom.

On 10 June 1912, shortly after the completion and testing of No. 4, Lt C.M. Waterlow of the RFC made an inspection. Admitting from a civilian viewpoint that both ships (No. 3 and No. 4) offered much promise, his conclusions were that 'While both ships would afford valuable training to Officers and men unacquainted with this class of work, they cannot seriously be considered for war purposes against a savage enemy'. Nevertheless, the Admiralty purchased No. 4 and its shed for £1,050 on 18 July 1912, and Willows No. 4 became HMA No. 2.

A handy little ship, HMA No. 2 was soon fitted with a new envelope and redesigned car with dual control, three seats and a 40 hp Renault engine. She carried out training duties into 1915. Her tail surfaces were removed and 'normal' elevator and rudder planes fitted to the rear of the envelope: eventually the only item remaining from the original Willows No. 4 was the swivelling-propeller gear!

HMA No. 2 was the last airship to fly out of Farnborough when operations moved to Kingsnorth on 26 January 1915. Although she never flew again, her envelope was used to build the first 'SS' ship (SS–1) by suspending a BE.2 aeroplane fuselage and engine from 'Eta' patches.

After No. 4's departure, in 1913 Willows built his last civilian airship in a canvas hangar on the Old Welsh Harp grounds at Hendon. This was the site of his approved aviation school which enabled students to obtain an airship pilot's licence for £100. The Willows No. 5 had a rubber-proofed fabric envelope of 50,000 cu ft and a 60 hp ENV 'F' 8-cylinder engine driving swivelling propellers. The pilot and passengers were seated in a streamlined car which contained the engine. This car had extended booms fore and aft and was suspended from a bridle. Attached to the stern of the envelope were the by-now standard elevator and rudder planes.

Little is known about No. 5's activities other than its participation in Hendon Air Pageants.

In October 1914 Willows was appointed chief engineer of Airships Ltd, a company formed by Holt Thomas in March 1914. When on 28 February 1915 the First Lord of the Admiralty, Lord Fisher, demanded 'an airship with a speed of 50 m.p.h., carrying two crew and wireless, 160 lb of bombs . . .', Airships Ltd, together with the Royal Naval Kingsnorth team and Messrs Short Bros, built a contender for this original 'SS' airship specification.

Officially numbered SS–2, it was in fact Willows' sixth airship. Produced in four weeks, it becomes obvious that much of the

Willows No. 1, Splot, Cardiff, 18 August 1905. The single propeller at the stern provided forward thrust while the two swivelling propellers in the bow could face outwards to change direction. (E.T. Willows)

Willows No. 2, Cardiff, early 1910.

Willows No. 3 taking off from Wormwood Scrubs on its cross-Channel flight, 4 November 1910. (E.T. Willows)

Willows No. 4 (HMA No.2), Farnborough, October 1912. It is shown here before it was modified by the Admiralty. Note *Beta* flying in the background. (E.T. Willows)

Willows No. 5 in flight. (Ces Mowthorpe Collection)

No. 1 or *Nulli Secundus* in her original form, being prepared for take off at Farnborough, 1907. (Ces Mowthorpe Collection)

Willows No. 5 design was incorporated. The car was almost identical with fore and aft booms, although a 100 hp Curtiss engine was coupled to swivelling propellers, while the 70,000 cu ft envelope of doped aeroplane fabric (which leaked badly) had the rudder and elevators at the rear. The porous and misshapen envelope did not impress the Royal Navy! Also, the otherwise excellent swivelling propeller system was difficult to mass produce. As a result the Royal Navy's contender, SS–1, was accepted into service. Although Airships Ltd's SS–2 was taken on charge, she appears to have been dismantled after appearing at Dover (Capel) on 9 April 1915.

In 1907 Col Capper, while in charge of the Royal Balloon Factory at Farnborough, received £2,000 from the Treasury to construct an Army airship. Assisted by his Chief Kiting Officer Samuel F. Cody, he constructed the officially named *Nulli Secundus*. This had an 111 ft long envelope, without a ballonet, of goldbeater's* skin, 18 ft in diameter and with a capacity of 56,000 cu ft. The envelope was covered with netting, from which hung a long spar and the car. The car was of triangular form with a movable elevator forward and a vertical rudder at the stern. A simple platform supported the crew and a 40 hp Antionette engine.

Taken out for the first time on 10 September 1907, *Nulli Secundus* made a captive ascent from the Farnborough Golf Course, followed by a short free flight. Two further flights, each of an hour's duration, took place at the end of the month.

* 'Goldbeater's skin' was made from thousands of oxen's intestines, cleaned and dried, then glued to a fine cloth backing and varnished. This formed the lightest possible gas-tight flexible envelope but was expensive and short lived. Its approximate life span was only three years before it became brittle. This material has been succeeded by specially developed patent rubber-based balloon fabrics.

On the morning of 5 October, *Nulli Secundus* departed Farnborough for London with Capper and Cody piloting. After circling Buckingham Palace and St Paul's cathedral, a course was set back to base. Unfortunately a rising head-wind greatly reduced the airship's ground-speed so it was deemed best to land on the Crystal Palace cycle track after a total flying time of three-and-a-half hours. Due to heavy rain, which damaged the goldbeaters skin envelope, the airship was transported back by road.

As a result of this experience, major alterations were carried out. These included increasing the capacity to 85,000 cu ft, enclosing both the envelope and keel with a waterproof silk covering, and attaching a 'Lebaudy'-style car containing the engine and crew to the keel. The airship now became *Nulli Secundus II* and first flew during July 1908, attaining a speed of 22 m.p.h. More flights took place during August 1908 but the craft was dismantled at the end of the month.

During the winter months of 1908 Col Capper built a smaller airship of 21,000 cu ft capacity. Unofficially christened *Baby*, it had a length of 84 ft and diameter of 24 ft. The envelope incorporated a ballonet and had inflated fins at the stern. After the first flight, these inflated surfaces were replaced by ordinary fixed planes. A rudimentary car contained two 10 hp Buchet engines driving a single propeller, which were later replaced by a 25 hp REP driving two propellers.

The spring of 1908 saw *Baby* make a number of flights, but she proved to be very unstable. A complete redesign was the only answer; this was carried out and she was renamed *Beta*.

Beta had a capacity of 35,000 cu ft and was powered by a 35 hp Green engine. The long car/keel was of triangular form with the centre portion covered in canvas. It had port and starboard outriggers to which the two chain-driven twin-bladed propellers were attached. Behind the engine sat the crew of two. An elevator was fitted forward and there was a vertical rudder in the usual stern position on the envelope. Horizontal planes complemented the rudder.

It could reasonably be claimed that *Beta* was the first truly efficient British service airship. After her maiden flight on 26 May 1910, she was the subject of many modifications, including being fitted with wireless. And being moored out to a portable mast in a 33 m.p.h. snowstorm during February 1912 did her no harm!

Despite her success, a complete reconstruction was undertaken in late 1912. When she emerged she was almost a different airship. Henceforth known as *Beta II* (and subsequently referred to as *Beta I* in her previous incarnation) she now had a goldbeaters skin envelope of 50,000 cu ft capacity, a modern-looking car without any extensions and a Clerget engine driving four-bladed propellers. The forward elevators were dispensed with; instead, movable surfaces were fitted to the horizontal tail-planes.

The new *Beta II* was operated to the full, being used for training and Army exercises, including night observation for the artillery. Following a major overhaul in July 1913 she was used by Capt E.M. Maitland for his experiments with parachutes, and after the outbreak of war she patrolled over London in 'defence of the capital'! With the new RNAS numbering system of January 1914, when the Navy took over all airships, *Beta II* became known as HMA No. 17.

December 1914 and January 1915 saw HMA No. 17 operational at Firminy, near Dunkirk, as part of the 'Dunkirk Squadron'. There she made several flights over enemy lines, once observing for the Belgian army's artillery.

Returning to base at Kingsnorth, she continued training wartime airshipmen,

before being shipped to Barrow during late 1915 for repairs. There she was fitted with a standard 'SS' envelope and may have returned to Pulham for training duties. She was finally struck off charge in 1916. Her car survives at the Science Museum, South Kensington.

Late in 1909 Col Capper designed and built a much larger airship than *Beta*, incorporating improvements from his earlier experiences. At this time he was in charge of the military wing at Farnborough, which was now under civilian control as the Aircraft Factory. Departing from previous practices, Capper ordered a 110,000 cu ft rubberised-cotton envelope from the Astra Airship Company of Paris. The car, with its extended framework, had elevators at either end, and contained the crew plus a 80 hp Green engine, which drove swivelling propellers through a gearbox and shafts made by Rolls-Royce.

The new airship's maiden flight took place on 12 February 1912. Despite a number of problems, she made numerous flights before being dismantled for major modifications. The Green engine was replaced by two 45 hp Iris motors, a box elevator at the stern of the car replaced the previous fore and aft pair, and a new envelope from Messrs Willows was fitted.

Now a successful operational airship, from June 1912 the new *Gamma* played her full part in service life. Fitted with a new envelope of 101,000 cu ft capacity in 1913, she then became known as *Gamma II*. When the Royal Navy renumbered airships in January 1914, *Gamma II* became HMA No. 18. Although superseded by more modern craft, HMA No. 18 remained in service until deflated and struck off charge in May 1916.

In 1912 Army manoeuvres saw the launch of another British airship. Named *Delta*, she was the largest to date. In her long gestation period, this 175,000 cu ft craft had already

Nulli Secundus II during trials at Farnborough, July 1908. (Ces Mowthorpe Collection)

Army airship *Baby* giving demonstration flights at Aldershot, 1909. (Ces Mowthorpe Collection)

Beta moored to a mast at Farnborough, February 1912. Note the rope ladder, which was climbed every half hour in order to inspect the gas content. The early car with its long open framework is clearly shown. (Ces Mowthorpe Collection)

Gamma (HMA No. 18) climbs out of Fort Grange, Portsmouth, using her swivelling propellers. Note the horizontal angle of the propellers. (Ces Mowthorpe Collection)

Army airship *Delta* (HMA No. 19), showing the original car, near Farnborough, 1912. (Ces Mowthorpe Collection)

Eta (HMA No. 20) at Farnborough, 1913. The two cockpits with the engine between can be easily made out. The propellers are at about 40° to the horizontal as the craft climbs away. (Ces Mowthorpe Collection)

been rebuilt, starting as a semi-rigid but finally emerging as a normal non-rigid. Her 28 ft long car contained the crew and two 105 hp White & Poppe engines driving swivelling propellers on port and starboard outriggers. Places were provided for up to five crew members.

Delta proved to be the fastest British airship to date, with a speed of 44 m.p.h. Using her swivelling propellers she could attain a vertical climb of 666 ft per minute without forward motion. However, on her fourth flight *Delta* had to make a successful single-engined return to Farnborough after one engine broke down over Norfolk. Later, her tail unit with horizontal and vertical planes and rudders underwent several changes, at one time an upper fin being fitted.

It was from this ship that Maj E.M. Maitland made his first parachute jumps, and during the 1913 manoeuvres the radio, permanently fitted, was notably efficient. Later, a new car, without extensions and partially enclosed, replaced the original.

Under the 1914 Naval numbering system *Delta* became HMA No. 19. Altogether an efficient airship, *Delta* was still in commission after the outbreak of the First World War.

The final British Army airship to be built was the *Eta*. This craft was the result of the six years of experiments and trials with the previous Army airships, and in *Eta* are to be found the basic roots of the First World War Royal Naval airships. Her suspension was innovative. Six rigging cables supported the car: each divided into two and then into three nearer to the envelope, dividing yet again into three. Finally the 36 cables were attached to the envelope by kidney-shaped adhesive patches which were stitched on. This method did away with netting and bridles, etc., spreading the load evenly over the envelope's surface. Known as 'Eta' patches, they were used, one way or another, on every British

non-rigid. They meant that there was no longer any need for the long extensions to the car or gondola previously used to prevent the envelope sagging. As a result, *Eta* had the first 'minimum-length' car, with seating for five, including the pilot: two sat forward and three at the rear. Between them was a pair of 80 hp Canton-Unne engines, each chain-driving a swivelling propeller on an outrigger.

With a capacity of 100,000 cu ft plus two ballonets, *Eta* proved very satisfactory. Her first flight was on 18 August 1913, and following her fourth to Odiham she towed HMA No. 2 back to Farnborough for repairs. In January 1914 *Eta* became HMA No. 20, and after war was declared carried out training duties and patrols over London 'in defence of the capital'.

HMA No. 20's end came in September 1914. After. taking off for Firminy, near Dunkirk, she force-landed at Redhill, suffering serious damage. She never flew again, and with other ex-Army ships was struck off charge in 1916.

Early in the war, a number of Astra-Torres airships were bought from France. One of them, No. 10, had a special car, reputed to have been built for a wealthy Belgian and rather luxurious! No. 10's tri-lobe envelope was used to build the first 'Coastal', C.1. During late 1915, several experiments were conducted at Farnborough using No. 10's car attached to the envelope of *Eta* (HMA No. 20). Officially known as *Eta 2*, flights were carried for several days from 9 January 1916. *Eta* was then dismantled and struck off charge.

During 1910, two airships were bought from France. The first to reach this country was the *Clement-Bayard II*: the *Daily Mail* had raised £6,000 for the construction of a shed at Wormwood Scrubs, and a private gift of another £5,000 enabled an order to be placed with the reputable and experienced Clement-Bayard Airship Co. Over 300 ft

Eta 2, Kingsnorth, January 1916. Only three or four flights were made. (Ces Mowthorpe Collection)

The Clement-Bayard airship, 1910. Bought from the French government, this was the first airship to cross the Channel. (Ces Mowthorpe Collection)

The Lebaudy (*Morning Post*) airship on its arrival at Farnborough after its cross-Channel delivery flight, 26 October 1910. (Ces Mowthorpe Collection)

long, with a cruising speed of 32 m.p.h., this ship was tested in the French Army's 1910 manoeuvres. Leaving Paris on 16 October 1910, it set course for Wormwood Scrubs. On board were Alphonse Clement, First Pilot Baudry, Second Pilot Leprince, Engineer Sabitier, and two mechanics, Dilasser and Daire. Arthur du Cros made the flight on behalf of the *Daily Mail*. The 246-mile flight was accomplished at 41 m.p.h., becoming the first airship flight from France to Britain.

While in the shed at Wormwood Scrubs her envelope leaked badly, causing a great dispute with the makers. Finally dismantled and taken to Farnborough, she never flew again.

The second French-built craft was constructed by Lebaudy-Freres of Soissons, another reputable airship builder. Sometimes it is referred to as the *Morning Post* airship because this newspaper raised £18,000 towards the cost. Powered by two 135 hp Panhard engines and capable of 34 m.p.h., it was Britain's largest airship to date. It was 337 ft long, with a diameter of 39 ft, and it had a capacity of 353,000 cu ft including three internal ballonets of 3,000 cu ft each. To house the 'Lebaudy', the War Office constructed a shed at Farnborough (subsequently known as the 'A' shed), allowing 10 ft clearance from the supplied dimensions. Unfortunately, no-one thought to notify the British authorities that the makers had increased the height of the airship by 9 ft 9 in!

On 26 October 1910 the Lebaudy airship crossed the Channel with a crew of seven, including Maj Bannerman, Col Capper's successor. Despite a slight head-wind, an average speed of 36 m.p.h. was maintained, easily outpacing an escorting French destroyer. Arriving at Farnborough five-and-a-half hours from take-off, the Lebaudy was being walked into the new shed when the officer-in-charge realised something was amiss! He called a 'halt', but his order was countermanded by a brigadier who was present. This resulted in the Lebaudy's envelope ripping on the shed roof and causing serious damage to the ship.

The shed clearance was raised, and on 4 May 1911 the airship was taken out for a trial flight. At 600 ft the Lebaudy became unmanageable and an emergency landing was made on the airfield. Out of control, she missed the landing party, crashing into a cottage on the boundary. Luckily no-one was badly hurt. After a dispute with the maker, the Lebaudy was finally scrapped.

From the foregoing it is apparent that, upon entry into the First World War, Britain had virtually no truly operational airship. Although *Beta*, *Delta* and *Eta* were practical airships, all lacked long-range capabilities. Fortunately the War Office had bought a French Astra-Torres and a German Parseval in 1912. Strictly speaking these come under the heading of pre-war ships, but their wartime operational records are extensive so they are discussed in the next chapter.

CHAPTER 2

ASTRA-TORRES AND PARSEVALS

In 1910–11 Spaniard Torres Quevedo designed a small non-rigid airship which was to have a far-reaching effect on Royal Naval airships. His main innovation was a trefoil-shape gas-bag, with the three lobes connected internally with porous fabric 'curtains'. This arrangement maintained the envelope's shape, making it much stiffer than an ordinary balloon-type envelope. The upper lobe had internal rigging hanging from either side. The two bottom lobes presented an almost flat undersurface, enabling the car or gondola to be slung much nearer to the envelope, thereby reducing drag.

On March 1911 this new airship flew to France, and was repaired by the French Astra Airship Company at Issy. From then on Astra adopted the trefoil envelope, resulting in the Astra-Torres airships.

In 1912 Britain's Committee of Imperial Defence ordered an Astra-Torres from France, along with other airships, namely from Parseval in Germany and Forlanini in Italy. (The Italian purchase never materialised.) Depending on completion of successful trials, a further two (later changed to three) airships would be bought.

HMA NO. 3

Numbered 3 under the new Admiralty system, the first Astra-Torres ship was the fourteenth to be built by the Astra firm and the second to employ the Torres envelope. No. 3 had a capacity of slightly over 280,000 cu ft, with three internal ballonets. The ship was powered by two Chenu engines, each driving a large two-bladed propeller mounted upon brackets high above the large enclosed box-shaped gondola.

No. 3's first flight was on 12 June 1913 at Farnborough, under the control of the French firm's pilots. At 2,000 ft one engine failed, the envelope lost shape due to the ballonet losing pressure, and a force landing had to be made. While being repaired, alterations were made to the tail-unit. Originally No. 3 had fixed stabilisers fitted to the 'lower' vertical fin (no upper fin was fitted). Vertical ascent was controlled by moving the whole gondola fore and aft, thus altering the centre of gravity. By the time she emerged from her shed on 8 September 1913, she had been modified by Royal Naval personnel to have moving elevators on the horizontal planes and an improved vertical rudder.

Still under the control of the French firm's pilots, No. 3 commenced her trials. By the end of the month she had completed them successfully, including a 6 hour flight around Portsmouth, the Isle of Wight, Bournemouth and Portland. She had also established a record speed, for a British airship, of 51.1 m.p.h.

Now in Royal Naval control, No. 3 became fully operational and together with the No. 4. (the Parseval airship) completed many flights before the outbreak of war. Her enclosed car made her a comfortable ship, and she was fitted with radio. Experiments with a portable mooring mast took place at Farnborough during spring 1914, and, together with No. 4, she carried out the first wartime patrols in and around the English Channel, including escorting troopships taking the British Expeditionary Force to France. Both airships flew from the new Royal Naval Air Station at Kingsnorth.

HMA No. 3 Astra-Torres secured to the mobile mooring-mast, Farnborough, spring 1914. Note the stationary propellers at the extreme ends of the pylons above the gondola. (Ces Mowthorpe Collection)

HMA No. 4 taking off, possibly at Farnborough, 1914. (JMB/GSL Collection)

HMA No. 8 Astra-Torres, Kingsnorth, spring 1915. (Ces Mowthorpe Collection)

Because No. 4 had less range, she patrolled the Straits of Dover while No. 3 flew further to the northeast, guarding the Channel approaches. With the BEF safely landed these patrols continued, but less intensively.

At this time, a detachment of RNAS aircraft and armoured cars went to defend the city of Ostend, and No. 3, under command of Wg Cdr N.F. Usborne accompanied them. Later they were evacuated to Dunkirk, where a photograph shows No. 3 moored to a portable mast, alongside Cdr Samson's famous 'Dunkirk Squadron' of heavier-than-air machines. From Dunkirk, No. 3 boldly flew reconnaissance flights to establish the extent of the German advance.

However, due to the vulnerability of airships to fire from the ground, No. 3 was soon returned to Kingsnorth. By now she had acquired what was to become the normal tail appendage for non-rigid airships, namely a vertical fin and rudder below the envelope, a fixed fin above the envelope and monoplane stabilisers and elevators in the horizontal plane. From Kingsnorth she carried out night flights over London to evaluate possible Zeppelin attacks, the last being on the 26 September 1914, when she also provided practice for searchlight crews.

During 1914 and early 1915, the Astra-Torres gave the Royal Navy much valuable experience, which served the service well for its later airship operations, but all this meant that No. 3 had to be withdrawn for a major overhaul in the summer of 1915. Due to more modern designs being in the pipe-line, her last flight was on 19 August 1915, prior to being laid up and deleted in May 1916.

HMA NOS. 8, 10 AND 16
As a result of the success of this first Astra-Torres, a further three were ordered from the French firm. These were delivered in 1914 and numbered No. 8, No. 10 and No. 16.

No. 8 (Astra-Torres No. XIX) was a sistership to No. 3 and she made her trials flight at Kingsnorth on 22 December 1914, piloted by Wg Cdr Usborne. Modifications were required, so the ship was deflated before making her second debut on 25 February 1915. Because No. 3 had been deflated and was being overhauled after her initial operations, No. 8 was placed under the command of Flt Cdr W.C. Hicks on 17 December 1914 and took over No. 3's operations in the Eastern Channel approaches until 11 May 1915. On 15 May, No. 3 resumed her operations and No. 8 was deflated, being deleted in May 1916.

The second ship of the new order, No. 10, Astra-Torres No. XVII, was slightly smaller than No. 3, having a capacity of 150,000 cu ft capacity and a smaller enclosed car. It appears doubtful that No. 10 ever flew after carrying out her trials in France. Subsequently her envelope was used to make 'Coastal' No. 1, and her car was rejected as being too heavy and complicated to mass-produce.

The third ship, No. 16, remains something of a mystery. Believed to be a sistership to No. 10, she was probably never assembled in her original form after trials in France. However, there is a record of experiments taking place at Farnborough during the First World War using a 'small Coastal envelope': perhaps this was No. 16's? No photographs of HMA.10, or HMA.16, have been traced.

Meanwhile, the peacetime success of the German Zeppelins had caused questions to be asked at the Admiralty. Clandestine visits and flights on the commercial Zeppelins were made to assess their performance, and the Royal Navy reviewed its own lighter-than-air operations. It even tried hard to buy a Zeppelin, but the German Government would not allow a sale.

Therefore the German Parseval company was approached, and again the German

Government tried to stop the sale. However, at this time Dr Parseval was not getting much support owing to the popularity of the Zeppelins, so he agreed to sell one of his latest large non-rigid designs, No. 18, to the Royal Navy. This became HMA No. 4, and a provisional order for three more (Parsevals Nos. 20, 21 and 22) was made. At the same time Vickers suggested building more Parsevals under licence.

P.18 (No. 4) was delivered to Farnborough in 1913, and proved so successful that the go-ahead for the other three ships was given. With the outbreak of war in August 1914 they were no longer available – in fact two already built by Parseval went to the German Navy! Instead, Vickers agreed to supply the missing ships (P.5, P.6 and P.7), but there was a long delay and they were not flown until November and December 1916.

It is obvious from photographs that the Nos. 6 and 7 were almost identical copies of the Parseval PL.25 which flew with the German Navy in late 1915. Therefore Vickers must have had plans of this later model prior to the outbreak of war. Why therefore was No. 5 different? A tentative suggestion is made that when the Navy wanted another Parseval to support No. 4, which was being used to train future rigid crews at Howden for the Rigid Trials Unit, the rather sophisticated PL.25-type car with its two Maybach engines was some way from completion. Hence a Parseval envelope was affixed to a much simpler and more easily made enclosed aluminium car, based on the 'Coastal' pattern. Despite years of research the writer has been unable to discover with certainty what engines were used. Certainly they were production types. B.G. Turpin suggests 240 hp Renaults, and this seems likely. Unfortunately, No. 5 (because of its design) did not have swivelling propellers, so was not as useful for rigid training as the other ships.

Strangely, its 'sistership', No. 6, spent six months in store at Barrow, prior to being sent to Howden. The reason given for this delay was a 'political' decision. Could the true reason be that No. 5 took much longer to produce than planned? No. 6 was almost ready for trials when No. 5 took to the air, so the subsequent delay in flying No. 6 may well have been just a face-saving exercise. The large number of flying hours completed by P.6, together with the nil operating hours of P.7, signify that P.7 was used exclusively for spares to keep P.6 in the air.

HMA NO. 4
Length: 312 ft
Diameter: 51 ft
Height: 70 ft
Speed: 43 m.p.h.
Capacity: 364,000 cu ft
Ballonets (2): 110,000 cu ft
Useful lift: 7,052 lb
Engines: Two 180 hp Maybach

No. 4 and her sisters Nos. 5, 6 and 7 were the largest British non-rigids until the coming of the 'North Sea' class. No. 4 was bought from Parseval Airship Co in 1912. Numbered PL.18 in the Parseval works series, she arrived at Farnborough together with four engineers from the Parseval works to show the Royal Navy crews how to assemble and operate the ship. All Parseval non-rigids of this period had a very pointed, streamlined envelope. The car was suspended by means of the Parseval trajectory suspension system which was designed to spread the load evenly over the whole envelope. This system also damped out uneven pitching movements. Powered by two engines, an unusual feature was her variable-pitch propellers, which had steel blades which could be changed in mid-air in case of a failure – assuming a spare blade was being carried! A machine-gun position, served by an access-tube, was fitted on the top of the envelope.

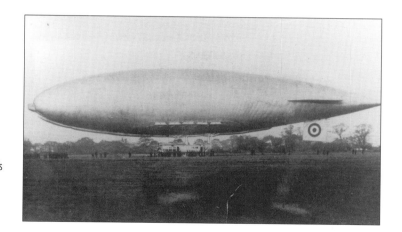

HMA No. 5 at Howden, being prepared for her trial flight, 12 November 1917. Note the gunner's position on the nose, which was known as the 'Howden Pulpit' and was a station modification. (JMB/GSL Collection)

HMA No. 5, Howden, with the 'modified Coastal' car, 12 November 1917. The trunking on the envelope carried air to the ballonets. The vertical tube on the car enabled the gunner to get to the 'Howden Pulpit'. (JMB/GSL Collection)

HMA No. 6 flying over the sheds at Howden, August 1917. (JMB/GSL Collection)

This airship carried out the first war patrols over the Thames Estuary, flying from Kentish Knock to Barrow Deep on 5 August 1914, commanded by Capt J.N. Fletcher. Returning in the early morning, No. 4 was fired upon by British Territorials, despite her White Ensign. At the same time, the War Office was plagued with reports of a German Zeppelin 'flying up the Thames'! No. 4 also escorted troopships carrying the BEF to France, protecting them from U-boats.

It was during one of these early patrols that No. 4 shed a propeller blade. As she carried a spare, this was refitted in mid-air while she drifted in the wind with engines stopped. Coxswain Cook, who was on board, later related that the wind carried them over the Belgian coast and it was dusk before the repair was completed. The crew could see flashes of gunfire on the Western Front.

During 1915, No. 4 was reconditioned by Vickers at Barrow. On 22 November she collided with a shed in dense fog, and later went from Pulham to Howden, where on 27 December 1916 she sustained slight damage on landing owing to a down gust. At Howden she was used for training Cdr Masterman's Rigid Trials Crew. On 24 March 1917 No. 4 returned to Pulham (captained by Flt Lt Moyes), where she was deleted on 17 July 1917.

HMA NO. 5
Length: 304 ft
Capacity: 364,000 cu ft
Ballonets (2): 110,000 cu ft capacity
Engines: possibly two 240 hp Renaults

No. 5 was the first of three 'Parsevals' built by Vickers at Barrow. Much assistance was initially given by Parseval because it had originally contracted to supply three further Parsevals (PL.20, PL.21 and PL.22) and Vickers was interested in building them under licence. However, on the outbreak of war

Vickers undertook to supply the Royal Navy with these three airships. Because of other priorities, construction soon was far behind schedule, none of the ships getting into service until late 1917.

So that they could be handled by inexperienced groundcrews, all three were specially strengthened, including steel strengtheners in the nose-cone. Ballast and fuel were carried in the car, along with a small petrol engine to drive the air-blower for inflating the ballonets. This could also be driven from either engine.

No. 5 was assembled at Howden and was the first one to be completed. She was fitted with a one-off car. Called a 'modified Coastal' car, it was in effect an enclosed 'Coastal' car, formed in aluminium, with an engine at each end. Following her trial flight on 12 November 1917 she was used for training rigid crews, with Flt Lt 'Tommy' Elmhirst captaining her on occasions. On 19 February 1918 she force landed at East Fortune and was deleted for spares at Howden on 9 July 1918. In total No. 5 flew 37 hours 37 minutes in 1917 and 69 hours 5 minutes in 1918.

HMA NO. 6
Length: 304 ft
Capacity: 364,000 cu ft
Ballonets (2): 110,000 cu ft
Engines: Two 180 hp Wolseley/Maybachs, driving swivelling propellers.

Built at Barrow, No. 6's trial flight took place on 17 December 1916. She was reassembled at Howden, having new trials on 15 June 1917 before being used by the Rigid Trials Unit at Howden. She was moved to Cranwell from Howden on 6 August 1917 and made a free-balloon landing at South Colton RFC aerodrome due to engine failure on 29 September 1917 (while captained by Lt Cdr Cooke). On 17 February 1918 she flew to

Pulham from Cranwell. In August she was in the No. 1 shed at Howden, together with R.27, C*3 and NS.9, when a 'spare' 'Zero', being rigged by an American crew, caught fire and destroyed itself plus the three aforementioned airships. Luckily P.6 survived through being in the upwind corner of the shed. The inrush of air caused by the conflagration rushed past her pointed streamlined envelope, feeding the flames but keeping P.6 relatively cool. Her survival in this inferno was regarded as little short of a miracle!

In March 1919 No. 6 was used for mine searching, before being deflated in May 1919 and deleted in October of the same year. In 1917 she had flown 113 hours, in 1918 294, and in 1919 another 81.

HMA NO. 7

Built Barrow and assembled at Howden (where her trials flight took place on 22 December 1917), P.7 was identical to P.6. Having been used for spares for P.6, she was deleted at Howden on 28 May 1918. It is possible that P.7 made a trials flight after being built at Barrow. No photograph of this airship can be located.

HMA No. 6, Howden, February 1918. Note the propellers on the out-riggers, as on No. 4. The top gunner reached his position by climbing along the top of the envelope using the ladder that led from the 'Howden Pulpit'. (JMB/GSL Collection)

CHAPTER 3

THE 'SEA SCOUTS'

THE 'SEA SCOUT' CLASS

On 28 February 1915, the Admiralty, under the First Lord, Lord Fisher, issued a specification for a small airship capable of searching for submarines in coastal waters. As we have seen on p. xx, its specification called for a 50 m.p.h. maximum speed and an endurance of 8 hours while carrying a crew of two, 160 lb of bombs and radio set with a range of 30 miles. Significantly, it would have to be capable of mass production.

When the Navy took over all airships in 1914, it transferred the lighter-than-air branch from Farnborough to the new RNAS Kingsnorth. A lot of airship expertise was available on construction and operation of non-rigids. Therefore the Navy set about building a ship to the Admiralty's specification. The new airship became known as the SS–1, Sea Scout 1 (although the names Submarine Searcher and Sea Searcher are sometimes used). The firm of Airships Ltd also built an airship, SS–2, to this specification, and Short Brothers, too, got an order which, had it been completed, would have been SS–3.

The team at Kingsnorth, commanded by Cdr Masterman, took a spare envelope from Naval Airship No. 2 (formerly Willows No. 4) and attached, by means of 'Eta' patches, an existing BE.2 aeroplane fuselage, less its wings and tail unit. The envelope had a capacity of only 40,000 cu ft and gave barely sufficient lift. It had been calculated that a minimum capacity of 60,000 cu ft would be required to fulfil the original specification.

Both SS–1 and SS–2 flew during March 1915, but the Short Bros design never left the drawing board. Despite its apparent shortcomings, SS–1 was adjudged the successful design after trials at Kingsnorth. Although SS–2 was soon deleted, Airships Ltd began manufacturing 'SS' class ships. At this time AIRCO, Airships' parent company, was manufacturing Maurice Farman aircraft under licence for the RFC, and so they produced an 'SS' variant utilising the Maurice Farman fuselage instead of the BE.2. Later, a further alteration took place when Armstrong-Whitworth FK.3 fuselages were adapted.

Many modifications were required to these aeroplane fuselage cars. The rudder pedals were retained for control in yaw but an elevator wheel was fitted for pitch control. In addition to the normal BE.2 9.5 gal gravity tank and the main 18 gal tank, a 32 gal tank was fitted beneath the fuselage, and provision for eight 16 lb bombs or a 112 lb bomb was made aft of the undercarriage. The car also had to carry 300 lb of water ballast and a grapnel and trail rope. The BE.2 and FK.3 fuselages had tractor engines, but the Maurice Farman had a pusher. Mainly the engines were 75 hp Renaults, but 100 hp Greens, 100 hp Berliets and on at least one occasion a 75 hp Rolls-Royce Hawk were later used.

The observer-W/T operator occupied the front cockpit, with the pilot flying the machine from the rear cockpit, except on the Maurice Farmans where the positions were reversed. Because they were 'pushers' and the crew were not in the slipstream, the Maurice Farman ships were favoured by crews, even

An unknown early SS-ship with a Maurice Farman-type car. Like the SS—23, this has been modified to take a third cockpit. (Ces Mowthorpe Collection)

SS—1, Kingsnorth, April 1915. Note the pointed nose and lack of nose-cone strengtheners. The BE.2c fuselage attached by 'Eta' patches became the prototype for SS-ships. (Ces Mowthorpe Collection)

SS—3 on trials prior to being dismantled and sent to the Middle East. The ship was built by Messrs. Short Bros. (Ces Mowthorpe Collection)

SS–2 (Willows V1), heavily modified for the RNAS, in the shed at Dover, 9 April 1915 (see text, p. 25). (The Royal Aeronautical Society)

though they were slightly slower. More Maurice Farman 'SS' ships survived the war than any other of this type.

The car was suspended from the envelope by ten main cables and two anti-rolling guys, which were attached to the envelope by 'Eta' patches. The envelope, which was 60,000 cu ft on the original production ships, incorporated a ripping panel for emergency deflation and two ballonets each of approximately 6,500 cu ft capacity, one forward, the other aft. They were inflated from a metal scoop mounted in the propeller slipstream. Two fabric non-return valves known to airshipmen as 'crab-pots' controlled the flow of air into and out of these ballonets. By adjusting pressure between these two ballonets, the envelope not only kept its shape but enabled the pilot to trim for various conditions of flight.

As well as factory modifications, many alterations took place at the various RNAS air stations, such as enlarging the fuselages to take an extra seat. Fuel tanks were eventually suspended in slings from the envelopes to increase their range, and the undercarriages were modified to suit the arrangement. The positioning of the 'vertical' fin or fins and rudder or rudders also varied. On Maurice Farman cars, dual control was fitted.

The result of all these modifications was to add extra weight, so the capacity of the envelope was eventually increased to 70,000 cu ft. Although the length of the new envelope remained the same, the diameter increased by approximately 3 ft.

Despite their many shortcomings, the 'SS' ships provided air cover when no other aircraft could do so. Being simple to fly, they gave the new generation of airshipmen first-class experience and prepared them for command of the improved airships which followed. Although a number were shipped to the Eastern Mediterranean theatre, they had not been designed for sub-tropical

operation and so their work there was limited. In particular, their lift was lessened by the climatic conditions, and the power and reliability of their engines was very variable. Fourteen of these small airships were also sold to Britain's wartime allies: ten to Italy and four to France.

The class number of a non-rigid airship in the RNAS always stayed with the car. No matter how many envelopes it used, the number of the ship remained the same. Only when the car was written off was an alteration made, e.g. C.23 became C.23A after the original car was damaged beyond repair in an accident on 1 May 1917.

THE 'SEA SCOUT' SHIPS

SS–1
Work commenced at Kingsnorth on 22 February 1915, rigging a BE.2c fuselage beneath the envelope of Willows No. 2. Commissioned at Kingsnorth 18 March 1915 as SS–1. Destroyed by fire after colliding with telegraph wires near Dover on 7 May 1915, when her pilot, Sub Lt Booth (who later commanded R.100) mistook the wind direction signal and landed down-wind. Both occupants escaped injury. Deleted Folkestone 7 May 1915, destroyed by fire.

SS–2
Built and designed by Airships Ltd, but proved unsatisfactory. Deleted. See Willows No. 6. The accompanying photograph shows SS–2 in the uncompleted shed at RNAS Capel near Folkestone. This photograph is from the Royal Aeronautical Society Library and is captioned as 'SS–2 in shed at Dover, 9 April 1915'. B.G. Turpin has SS–2's first flight on 5 May 1915 at Kingsnorth. Such contradictions make it difficult to arrive at accurate histories of the airships now that most of the evidence has disappeared!

SS–4, Folkestone, summer 1915. Note the 'saddle-seat' on the fuselage behind the pilot's cockpit. This was used by an instructor when training the pilot. Note also the use of airbags as opposed to wheels on the undercarriage. (Ces Mowthorpe Collection)

SS–5 being towed to shore by a destroyer after a forced landing in the sea, 11 November 1915. (Ces Mowthorpe Collection)

SS–8 descending. (Fleet Air Arm Museum; neg. no. A/SHIP/251)

The car of SS–6, showing the third cockpit, which was a station modification. Compare it with the detachable 'jump' seat of the SS–4. (Fleet Air Arm Museum; neg. no. A/SHIP/63)

SS–7 being walked out of the shed at Kingsnorth, possibly for trials. (Fleet Air Arm Museum; neg. no. A/SHIP/352)

SS–3
BE.2c car. Sent to Imbros in 1915 as part of the Airship Expeditionary Force. At Mudros 16 March 1916. Deleted Mudros 19 April 1918, unserviceable.

SS–4
BE.2c car. To Folkestone 8 May 1915. Packed at Wormwood Scrubs 10 August 1917. Dispatched to Italian Government 4 September 1917. Assembled Grottaglie by Capt Meager 12 January 1918.

SS–5
BE.2c car. To Folkestone 1915. Climbed to 10,000 ft in 25 minutes from Polegate, reaching a maximum height of 10,350 ft while piloted by a Sub Lt McEwan. Made forced landing in Channel 11 November 1915. To Italian Government from Wormwood Scrubs 14 July 1917. Assembled Grottaglie by Capt Meager 9 November 917.

SS–6
BE.2c car. To Polegate 1915. To Italian Government from Wormwood Scrubs 14 July 1917. Assembled Grottaglie by Capt Meager 6 January 1918.

SS–7
BE.2c car. Arrived Imbros-Kassandra 13 September 1915 as a part of the Airship Expeditionary Force. Carried out artillery spotting for HMS *Venerable* and HMS *Talbot* 25/26 September 1915. Deleted Kassandra 19 April 1918, unserviceable.

SS–8
BE.2c car. To Folkestone from Kingsnorth 17 December 1915. To Mudros 18 July 1916 as part of the Airship Expeditionary Force. To Kassandra 17 December 1916. For full performance of this airship see p. 607 CB/819/1918 (Airship Expeditionary Force 2). Deleted Kassandra 19 April 1918, unserviceable.

SS–9
BE.2c car. To Polegate 1915. On 7 August 1916 conducted W/T tests with No. 9r, which could be heard at Longside, 460 miles away. Deleted Polegate 13 September 1916, replaced by SS–9A. To Polegate from Folkestone. To Howden 3 February 1917. Forced landing at Middleton-on-the-Wolds in snowstorm 4 December 1917. Polegate from Howden 5 January 1918. Deleted Polegate 15 June 1918, unserviceable. Packed and dispatched to Pulham 15 June 1918 for mooring mast experiments with Kingsnorth mooring. Moored out in September for 100 hours 15 minutes.

SS–10 AND SS–10A
BE.2c car. To Folkestone. Commissioned May 1915. To Marquise from Folkestone 26 August 1915. Wrecked in Channel 10 September 1915. Deleted Folkestone 10 September 1915, replaced. Reconstructed Folkestone as SS–10A. Deleted Folkestone 2 February 1916, replaced.

SS–10B
To Italian Government from Wormwood Scrubs 2 June 1917. Assembled Grottaglie by Capt Meager 19 January 1918.

SS–11
BE.2c car. To Capel September 1916 (captained by Sub Lt G. Meager). To Italian Government from Wormwood Scrubs 4 September 1917. Assembled Grottaglie by Capt Meager 31 December 1917.

SS–12
BE.2c car. To Folkestone 1915 (captained by Midshipman – later Air Marshal, RAF – Victor Goddard). Said by Air Marshal Goddard to have been the car of SS–1 fitted with a new envelope. Deleted 4 March 1917, replaced by new type.

SS–13 AND SS–14A

BE.2c car. To Folkestone 1915. On 29 March 1916 Sub Lt W.P.C. Chambers and Midshipman Victor Goddard carried out night-flying tests at Capel. To Polegate from Folkestone 4 May 1916 for further night-flying tests. Sir Brian Leighton jumped with Calthorpe parachute 5 August 1916. Force landed in sea off Eastbourne 29 April 1917. Towed to Newhaven and salvaged. From Wormwood Scrubs dispatched to Pulham 25 September 1917. <u>October 1917 renumbered 14A.</u> Damaged in gust 13 October 1917. Deflated Pulham 23 January 1918. Re-inflated and fitted with a Rolls-Royce 75 hp Hawk engine. To Luce Bay February 1918. Experimentally fitted with fin and rudder on top of envelope. Took part in mooring experiments at Pulham on 4 September 1918, being moored to a single-wire system. Arguably the longest-serving airship in the wartime RNAS. Deleted September 1919. SS–14A flew 13 hours 3 minutes in 1918.

SS–14

BE.2c car. At Kingsnorth June 1916. Fitted with water-cooled Curtiss engine. Capt E.E. Taylor. To Laira. Engine failure, ballooned over Channel to France on 7 September 1917. Rebuilt Kingsnorth and fitted with a Rolls-Royce Hawk 75 hp engine. Deleted Kingsnorth 1 May 1918, unserviceable.

SS–15

BE.2c car. To Marquise 9 August 1915. To Wormwood Scrubs from Marquise 19 December 1915. To Pembroke from Wormwood Scrubs 25 April 1916. First airship to operate from RNAS Pembroke. Deleted Pembroke 18 January 1917, wrecked off Lundy Isle.

SS–16

BE.2c car. To Polegate 1915 and 1917. In September 1917 made a flight of 44 hours 55 minutes. Deleted Wormwood Scrubs 11 May 1918, unserviceable.

SS–17

BE.2c car. To Luce Bay 1915. Flown by Sub Lt Elmhirst during summer 1915. On one occasion the rudder cables came adrift and, with the crew unable to make repairs, SS–17 and crew drifted across the Irish Sea to carry out a successful balloon landing in Ireland – but only after jettisoning all 'unnecessary' equipment, including the compass and W/T set. To Kassandra 28 June 1916 as part of the Airship Expeditionary Force 2. Was inflated in the newly erected airship shed at Mudros, on the island of Lemnos, in the Aegean. However this shed was bombed nightly by Turkish aircraft, so, after only a few flights, SS–17 was deflated and dispatched to the shed at Kassandra. Sighted U-boat in Aegean Sea in August 1916. SS–17 was wrecked in the sea off Kassandra in 1917. Replaced by SS–19. The shed at Mudros continued to be used by aeroplanes and acquired the nickname of the 'Pepper-pot'. Deleted Kassandra 19 April 1918, unserviceable.

SS–18

BE.2c car. To Anglesey 26 September 1915 (captained by F/Sub Lts W. Urquart and Kilburn. Carried away undercarriage while landing and drifted out to sea, finally coming down off Ireland 22 October 1916 – totally lost with one rating drowned. Deleted Anglesey 9 November 1916, lost at sea. No photograph of SS–18 can be traced.

SS–19

BE.2c car. To Imbros 1915 aboard SS *Joshua Nicholson*, as part of the Airship Expeditionary Force. To Mudros 16 March 1916. Deleted Mudros 19 April 1918, unserviceable. Records show that SS–19 was erected and flown from the Kassandra shed after the loss of SS–17 in 1917. Her captain was Flt Lt 'Bird' Irwin.

A movie camera aboard what is believed to be SS—9 at Polegate, 1915. (The Royal Aeronautical Society)

SS—10 comes down in the Channel, 10 September 1915. Her trail-rope is being taken to a trawler. The SS—10 was rebuilt as the SS—10A. (Fleet Air Arm Museum; neg. no. A/SHIP/211)

SS—11, on the right, flying in formation with four other ships. At the time this type of flying was known as 'Fleet tactics'. (JMB/GSL Collection)

SS—12 entering the shed at Capel, 10 August 1915. (JMB/GSL Collection)

SS—13, renumbered SS—14A, late 1917. Note the undercarriage; by this time it was standard for SS-ships to have 'skids' rather than wheels. (Ces Mowthorpe Collection)

SS—14 taking off. (Ces Mowthorpe Collection)

The maiden flight of SS—17, piloted by Sub Lt T.W. Elmhirst, 3 July 1915. This was the first Barrow-built airship to fly successfully. She was sent by rail to Stranraer on 15 July — followed by SS—23 — when Luce Bay Airship Station became operational. (JMB/GSL Collection)

What is believed to be SS—19, taking off from Mudros, 1916. (JMB/GSL Collection)

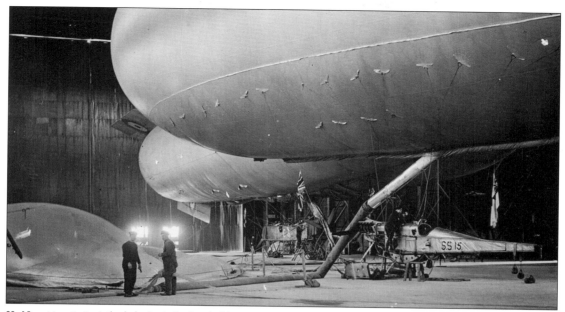

SS–15 receiving attention in the shed at Pembroke. Note the fabric piping, from an external blower for maintaining ballonet pressure. 'Coastal' C.3 is in the background. (Fleet Air Arm Museum; neg. no. A/SHIP/349)

SS–16 being walked out of the shed. (Fleet Air Arm Museum; neg. no. A/SHIP/66)

SS–20
BE.2c car. To Luce Bay 1915. Deleted Wormwood Scrubs 17 July 1918, unserviceable.

SS–21
BE.2c car. Sold to French Government for approximately £2,500 and numbered VH–1. No photograph of SS–21 has been traced.

SS–22
BE.2c car. To Anglesey 5 November 1915, captained by F/Sub Lt E.F. Turner. Reputed to have dived from 1,100 ft to 100 ft in 56 seconds. To Wormwood Scrubs from Anglesey April 1917. To Italian Government from Wormwood Scrubs 2 June 1917. Assembled at Grottaglie by Capt Meager August 1917. After engine failure on 2 September 1917 her Italian crew jumped out when near the ground but SS–22 thus lightened rose to 10,000 ft. Three Nieuport fighters shot it down, but on landing it was little the worse for wear except the envelope, which was full of bullet holes. No photograph of SS–22 can be traced.

SS–23
BE.2c car. To Luce Bay 1915. Force landed, engine unserviceable and envelope ripped near Girvan on 21 November 1916. Landed on Anglesey beach near Red Wharf in gale, held for 3 hours then envelope ripped on 2 January 1917. Deleted Luce Bay 1 May 1918, unserviceable.

SS–24
BE.2c car. To Anglesey 1915, captained by Sub Lt Scroggs. To Luce Bay from Anglesey 11 July 1917. Deleted Wormwood Scrubs 17 July 1918, unserviceable.

SS–25
BE.2c car. To Anglesey 1915, captained by T.B. Williams. Force landed, car and planes damaged 23 November 1917. Deleted Anglesey 15 March 1918, replaced by new type. Flew 149 hours August–December 1917; 77 hours 24 minutes 1918.

SS–26
To Folkestone from Polegate 17 December 1915. To Marquise from Polegate for French Government 28 December 1915 and numbered VH–2. No photograph of SS–26 can be traced.

SS–27
Armstrong FK car. Built by Armstrong-Whitworth. To Marquise 8 July 1915. Wrecked in collision with church steeple at Marquise 5 August 1915. Deleted Marquise 5 August 1915, wrecked. No photograph of SS–27 can be traced.

SS–28
Maurice Farman car. Built at Folkestone. To Folkestone 1915. To Pulham from Barrow 1 February 1917. Deleted Cranwell 12 March 1918, replaced.

SS–28A
Maurice Farman car. Rebuilt at Cranwell. To Pulham September 1917. At Cranwell all 1918 and until May 1919. Hours flown 1917–19: 978 hours. Deflated 23 May 1919. Deleted October 1919.

SS–29
Maurice Farman car. Built at Folkestone. To Folkestone 1915. Escorted the King on visit to France and return 3 July 1917 and 14 July 1916. Cranwell from Folkestone 11 December 1917 captained by Edward Broome. Force landed at Ranceby due to engine failure 3 January 1918. Took part in mooring trials at Pulham with rollers. Hours flown 1917–18: 685 hours. Deflated Cranwell 27 January 1919. Deleted September 1919.

This is possibly SS–20, approaching to land at Luce Bay, 1915. (Ces Mowthorpe Collection)

SS–23, Luce Bay, September 1915. Note the modification for the third cockpit cut out in the rear fuselage. (Ces Mowthorpe Collection)

SS–24 landing at Barrow, 8 August 1915. The handling-crew have hold of the forward guys and are running to grab hold of the ship when she touches down. (Ces Mowthorpe Collection)

SS–25, Anglesey, December 1916. The airship has a BE-type car. The pilot was Sub Lt T.B. Williams. (Ces Mowthorpe Collection)

SS–28, Cranwell, 20 March 1918. Note the latest style 'vertical' air-scoop, fitted retrospectively. This airship was rebuilt as SS–28A, and is arguably the longest-serving RNAS SS airship. Total hours flown: 978. (Ces Mowthorpe Collection)

SS–30
Maurice Farman car. Built at Kingsnorth. To Polegate 27 November 1916. Force landed at Beachy Head. Complete car dispatched to Cranwell 20 March 1917. Deleted Polegate 23 October 1917, replaced.

SS–30A
Maurice Farman car. Rebuilt at Cranwell. Hours flown 1917–18: 807 hours. Deflated Cranwell January 1919. Deleted September 1919.

SS–31
Maurice Farman car. Built at Kingsnorth. Trials 26 September 1916. Sub Lt T.B. Williams' first command. To Cranwell December 1916. Collided with roof of rigid shed and made free balloon landing 3 miles away 11 July 1917. Deleted Cranwell 2 November 1917. Replaced.

SS–31A
Maurice Farman car. Rebuilt at Cranwell. Hours flown 1918: 665 hours. Deflated January 1919. Deleted September 1919.

SS–32
Maurice Farman car. Built at Barrow. Trials 10 April 1916. To Folkestone 1916. Deleted Folkestone 10 October 1916, replaced.

SS–32A
Maurice Farman car. Rebuilt at Barrow. Fitted with 85,000 cu ft envelope and airbag floats. Experimented landing and taxying on water at Barrow 23 April 1917. Moored at sea 26 April 1917. Wrecked in gusts of 30 m.p.h. at 11.30 hours 5 May 1917. Further experiments carried out, with the engine removed, in the Cavendish Dock. Moored for six days to a mast on a raft, 26 November 1917, in gusts up to 35 m.p.h. Wheels were now fitted to the floats and a 'mooring cone' fitted to the envelope for mooring purposes. Finally wrecked in 42 m.p.h. gusts when mooring cone torn out of envelope 6 March 1918. Mooring experiments July–November 1917. Deleted Barrow 17 July 1917, unserviceable.

SS–33
Maurice Farman car. Built at Barrow. To Luce Bay from Barrow 1916. To Anglesey from Luce Bay 4 November 1916. Force landed at Cemlyn Bay due to engine failure April 1917 – only slight damage. Deleted Wormwood Scrubs, replaced. No photograph of SS–33 can be traced.

SS–34
Maurice Farman car. Built at Barrow. Trials 30 January 1916. To Barrow 1915. Fitted with car from *Beta* 30 January 1916. On 16 February 1916 was damaged when shed blew down. Re-rigged to Maurice Farman car, trials with car 2 August 1916. Fitted with Nieuport seaplane floats. Mooring experiments including to raft in Cavendish Dock. Envelope destroyed in gale 5 May 1917. Deleted Barrow 5 May 1917.

SS–35
Maurice Farman car. Built at Wormwood Scrubs. Pulham from Wormwood Scrubs 14 November 1917. Hours flown 1917–18: 42 hours 57 minutes. Deflated 22 February 1919. Deleted Pulham September 1919.

SS–36
Maurice Farman car. Built at Wormwood Scrubs. To Pulham from Barrow by rail 24 July 1918. Mooring test (120 hours) to the semi-circular yoke of the Masterman Mast September 1918. Deleted 9 January 1919.

SS–37
Maurice Farman car. To Folkestone 1915. To Pembroke 7 March 1917. Dispatched to Cranwell May 1917. Force landed through engine failure at Harpswell, 12 miles north of

SS–29, Capel, 22 October 1916. (Ces Mowthorpe Collection)

SS–31 with a modified Maurice Farman car, Kingsnorth, August 1916. This was used as an experimental ship, and was piloted by Sub Lt T.B. Williams. (Ces Mowthorpe Collection)

SS–34 (without an engine) in Cavendish Docks, Barrow, 11 July 1917. This was the only SS-ship fitted with floats rather than airbags. She was used for mooring experiments on water. (Ces Mowthorpe Collection)

SS–30A with her rebuilt and modified car, Cranwell, 1918. (The Royal Aeronautical Society)

SS–32A (with airbag floats and no engine) moored to the Masterman Mast at Walney Island, 4 May 1918. (Ces Mowthorpe Collection)

Lincoln, on 14 January 1918. Deleted Cranwell 14 January 1918, replaced.

SS–37A

Hours flown: 372 hours 1917–19. Deflated 15 May 1919. Deleted September 1919.

SS–38

Maurice Farman car. Built at Wormwood Scrubs. To Luce Bay. Force landed in sea 25 January 1917. Salvaged, and envelope used on SS–23. Deleted Luce Bay 2 February 1917, lost at sea. No photograph of SS–38 can be traced.

SS–39

Maurice Farman car. To Cranwell from Wormwood Scrubs on delivery flight 15 November 1916. Wrecked by defective valve causing uncontrolled descent. Force landed in tree 12 May 1917. Broke away from landing party 25 July 1917; Wg Cdr Waterlow failed to release handling-guy and was killed. Deleted Cranwell 30 September 1917, replaced. No photograph of SS–39 can be traced.

SS–39A

Armstrong car. Rebuilt at Cranwell. Trials 1 October 1917. Hours flown 1917–18: 300 hours. Deflated 29 January 1919. Deleted Cranwell September 1919.

SS–40

Armstrong car with 100 hp Green engine, specially silenced. Built at Wormwood Scrubs. Modified for special night flights over enemy lines at Kingsnorth. Trials 26 May 1916. Demonstrated to War Office representatives at Polegate on night of 30 May 1916. To France (Marquise) from Polegate 6 July 1916 with black envelope (70,000 cu ft). To Boubers-sur-Canche 7 July 1916, captained by Sub Lt W.P.C. Chambers and Midshipman Victor Goddard. To Kingsnorth 8 August 1916 to have new larger black envelope fitted (85,000 cu ft). Back to Boubers-sur-Canche 10 August 1916. Parachute experiments with Lt Robbins and carrier pigeons 15 August 1916. Experimental night reconnaissance carried out over enemy lines and Somme battlefield during August and September 1916. Kingsnorth 22 October 1916. Pembroke 24 March 1917. Deflated at Wormwood Scrubs August 1917. To Kassandra (Airship Expeditionary Force 4). Deleted Kassandra 1 October 1918, unserviceable.

SS–41

Armstrong car. Built at Wormwood Scrubs. To Kingsnorth from Wormwood Scrubs 3 July 1916. To Caldale from Kingsnorth by rail 20 July 1916. First flight Caldale 20 August 1916. To Caldale December(?). Deleted Wormwood Scrubs 11 May 1918, unserviceable.

SS–42

Armstrong car. Built at Wormwood Scrubs. To Pembroke. Trials 28 August 1916. Broke away after landing with pilot (Flt Lt E.F. Monk) aboard, and ballooned with car inverted for a 100 miles, rising to 8,000 ft with the pilot hanging precariously on the undercarriage, before crashing at Ivybridge in Devonshire; Flt Lt Monk was unhurt. Wrecked 15 September 1916.

SS–42A

Rebuilt at Wormwood Scrubs. To Pembroke August 1917. Crashed into farm during night landing. Drifted out to sea and wrecked. F/Sub Lt Cripps and W/T operator lost. Deleted Pembroke 12 September 1917, lost at sea.

SS–43

Armstrong car. Built at Wormwood Scrubs. To Kingsnorth from Wormwood Scrubs 9 July 1916. Caldale from Kingsnorth by rail 20 July 1916. First flight 24 August 1916. Deleted Wormwood Scrubs 11 May 1918, unserviceable. No photograph of SS–43 can be traced.

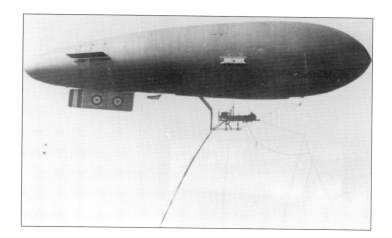

SS–35 undertaking mooring experiments, 27 April 1918. (JMB/GSL Collection)

SS–36 at the Masterman-type mooring-mast, September 1918. Note the long linen tube from the air-scoop to the compressor maintaining the ballonet pressure. (JMB/GSL Collection)

SS–37 landing at Cranwell, 1917. (Fleet Air Arm Museum; neg. no. A/SHIP/367)

SS–40 at Kingsnorth, August 1916, after being fitted with the larger envelope for night operations over the Western Front. Note the extra large fin to compensate. (Ces Mowthorpe Collection)

What is believed to be SS–41 at Caldale, mid-1917. Note the enlarged (possibly 80,000 cu ft) envelope, which requires an extra fin. (Ces Mowthorpe Collection)

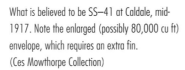

SS–42 taking off for patrol from Pembroke, August 1916. Note the 2-cylinder fuel tanks slung above the car. Below the car are grapnel and trail-rope (aft) and bomb (forward). (JMB/GSL Collection)

SS–44

Armstrong car. Built at Wormwood Scrubs (cost approximately £3,000). Crashed into trees and fence at Wormwood Scrubs while piloted by Italian, Cdr Dente; Lt Baldwin RNVR, thrown out, pilot trapped in car and carried in inverted position to a great height, finally came down in Walthamstow, where Cdr Dente's arm was broken. To Italian Government. No photograph of SS–44 can be traced.

SS–45

Armstrong car. Built at Wormwood Scrubs. To Italian Government. No photograph of SS–45 can be traced.

SS–46

Armstrong car. Built at Wormwood Scrubs. To Italian Government. No photograph of SS–46 can be traced.

SS–47

Armstrong car. Built at Wormwood Scrubs. To Italian Government. No photograph of SS–47 can be traced.

SS–48

BE.2c car. Built at Wormwood Scrubs, approximate cost £2,500. To French Government, numbered VH–3. No photograph of SS–48 can be traced.

SS–49

BE.2c car. Built at Wormwood Scrubs. To French Government, numbered VH–4. No photograph of SS–49 can be traced.

AP–1

This was an anti-Zeppelin experiment which consisted of an 'SS'-type envelope which had a complete BE.2c aircraft slung beneath by a quick-release harness. AP stood for Airship Plane. The idea was that the BE.2c could be released at about the same height as the Zeppelin. This meant the BE.2c did not have to climb, then intercept and attack. The first release, without a crew, was successful. On 21 February 1916, Cdr N.F. Usborne and Lt Cdr de Courcy W.P. Ireland carried out a full-scale test. Unfortunately the release mechanism became entangled and the aircraft inverted, plunging to earth from a low altitude. Both occupants were thrown out and killed. Thereafter the Admiralty banned all further experiments and AP–2, although completed, never flew. The serial number of the BE.2c was 989.

AP–1, the 'airship-plane' designed by Cdr W.P. Ireland and Cdr Usborne, being test-flown by Lt Hicks at Kingsnorth, August 1915. (Ces Mowthorpe Collection)

CHAPTER 4

THE 'COASTALS' AND 'COASTAL STARS'

THE 'COASTAL' CLASS

While the 'SS' class had been hurriedly developed at Kingsnorth on Admiralty instructions, the practical airshipmen in the RNAS realised that these little ships were only a stop-gap, with obvious limitations. What was needed was a larger airship with greater range and twin-engined reliability. Therefore a team at Kingsnorth began to develop the 'Coastal' class of airship.

They designed the car around obsolescent aircraft fuselages, as had been done for the 'SS' ships. They acquired one of the RNAS's twin-cockpit Avro 510 seaplanes, No. 131, with its relatively reliable Sunbeam 150 hp water-cooled engine. With the assistance of Avro personnel, the tapered tail was removed aft of the cockpits and replaced with a similar portion, including another 150 hp Sunbeam but with a pusher airscrew. The result was a four-cockpit car, with a 150 hp Sunbeam at either end, one a tractor, the other a pusher. And, being of aircraft construction, it could easily be mass-produced.

This car was rigged to No. 10's envelope – which, incidentally, was still in its original chrome-yellow colour – and made its first trial flight on 26 May 1915 at Kingsnorth. At this stage the car retained the legs for supporting the original seaplane floats, but they were removed after the initial landing. Subsequently the 'Coastal' was given conspicuous fore and aft single skids, attached to the original float leg points. The

horizontal stabilisers and elevators were also fitted to the upper surface of the bottom lobes on the envelope, rather than the higher position of No. 10. Further flights in May brought more modifications, such as strengtheners to the nose cone and alterations to the radiator of the aft engine. Thus was the 'Coastal' class of non-rigid airship born. The approximate cost of each 'Coastal' airship was £7,000.

All the early 'Coastals' had their air-scoop to the ballonets immediately abaft the forward propeller, but this proved awkward when used operationally: in a heavy landing it swung into and shattered the forward propeller, also causing serious damage to the envelope. As it also obstructed the coxswain's forward vision, on later ships it was installed just forward of the after propeller, the alteration being made retrospectively to the earlier craft.

As we have seen, the original car held a crew of four. The coxswain occupied the front cockpit, with the pilot behind him. Next came the wireless operator's cockpit, which contained a small ABC petrol engine for working his set, and by switching belts, could be used to power the auxiliary blower for the ballonets. The engineer's cockpit was aft, next to the rear engine. From late 1917, provision was made to carry six static-line parachutes, the crews wearing harnesses during each flight.

Between the pilot's and wireless operator's seats there was a space in which a large canvas bag of water ballast was carried. This was often done away with and a fifth cockpit installed for an observer/passenger. Instead, pilots would use fuel and bombs as emergency ballast, with small bags of sand, slung outboard of the car, for minor alterations of trim.

On the early 'Coastals', the fuel was carried in cylindrical tanks on brackets above the car. Soon, however, crews adopted what became normal RNAS practice, namely slinging fuel tanks on either side of the envelope. The Sunbeams were later upgraded to 160 hp, but reliability was not their strong point. Later 'Coastals' had 220 hp Renaults fitted aft and 100 hp Berliets or Greens forward.

As well as these 'official' design changes, many RNAS war stations carried out non-standard but essentially practical modifications.

The envelopes were frequently changed due to accident damage and wear and tear. However, by late 1918 the British rubber-based envelope was proving to be relatively long-wearing. For example, C.23A's envelope had a recorded life of nearly 1,000 hours of continuous inflation – admittedly a figure recorded because it was by then almost unusable and should have been changed months before.

When fully loaded, the 'Coastals' could carry nearly half-a-ton of bombs or depth bombs for a 10–12 hour patrol. Maximum speed was 45–47 m.p.h. and endurance was over 20 hours. At first disliked by the crews, with experience the 'Coastals' proved the workhorses of the RNAS's lighter-than-air division throughout the First World War.

The 'Coastals' were armed with two Lewis guns for self-protection. One could be attached to various mountings on the car, the other was on an upper gun platform. Access to this platform was up a 30 inch diameter tube, which went completely through the centre of the envelope and terminated in a wooden trapdoor near the top. Once through this, the gunner stood on the trap and operated a Lewis gun on a Scarff mounting attached to a wood frame laced to the top of the envelope. Although the top gun was little used in the early years, the loss of C.17 in April 1917 led to all 'Coastals' flying more than 3 miles from land being ordered to have it manned at all times – even to the extent of carrying an extra member to act as gunner.

THE 'COASTAL' SHIPS

Length: 196 ft overall
Capacity: 170,000 cu ft
Engines: One 150 hp Sunbeam (tractor), one 220 hp Renault (pusher)
Armament: Two machine-guns, one on top of envelope, four 112 lb or two 230 lb bombs or depth charges

C.1

Built at Kingsnorth. Trial flights 26 May 1915. Capt I. McDonald 12–16 May 1916. First flight as C.1 26 May 1916. Remained at Kingsnorth for development and experimental work. On-tow at Harwich by light cruiser HMS *Carysfoot* 12 May 1916. After experiments at Kingsnorth C.1 carried out refuelling and interchange of crews with HMS *Canterbury* 6 September 1916. Deleted Kingsnorth 1 June 1918, unserviceable. Prototype: Astra-Torres tri-lobe envelope from No. 10 (modified), and in its original undoped yellow colour. Two 150 hp Sunbeam engines.

C.2

Built at Kingsnorth. First flight September 1915. Retained for experiments. Trials 28 January 1916. To Mullion from Kingsnorth by rail 1 April 1917. Inflated 5 April 1917. To Howden from Mullion via Pulham and Kingsnorth 13 December 1918. Captain from

C.1 at Kingsnorth, showing the original 150,000 cu ft envelope from Astra-Torres No. 10. Note the new strengthening strips showing up on the chrome yellow coloured envelope. (Ces Mowthorpe Collection)

C.2 on patrol from Mullion. (JMB/GSL Collection)

C.4 landing at Howden. (Ces Mowthorpe Collection)

C.3 at Pembroke. (S.E. Taylor via Brian Turpin)

C.6 at Pembroke. (S.E. Taylor via Brian Turpin)

October 1918 until April 1919 was Lt A.E. McEwan. Hours flown: 88 hours 15 minutes 1916, 771 hours 24 minutes 1917, 1,414 hours 14 minutes 1918. C.2 was one of the outstanding 'Coastals'. When finally deleted in 1919, C.2 had averaged 3 hours flying per day over two-and-a-half years!

C.3

Built at Kingsnorth. Pembroke from Kingsnorth 9 June 1916. Kingsnorth from Pembroke 20 March 1918. Deleted Kingsnorth 31 August 1918, replaced by new type. Hours flown: 198 hours October–December 1917, 208 hours 49 minutes 1918.

C.4

Built at Kingsnorth. Trials 5 March 1916. Left for France, renumbered Ce, 23 April 1916. Transferred to French Air Force and renumbered AT–0 (Astra-Torres Zero). Delivered by air to Le Havre. New 'Coastal' numbered C.4. Trials Kingsnorth April 1916. To Howden from Kingsnorth by rail June 1916. First operational flight 3 July 1916. To Longside from Howden via East Fortune 7 September 1918. Damaged rudder plane at Howden November 1917. March 1918 at Howden (captained by Flt Lt Crouch). Hours flown: 252 hours 50 minutes 1916, 528 hours 1917, 697 hours 1 minute 1918. Deflated Longside 21 January 1919. Deleted October 1919.

C.5

Built at Kingsnorth. Trials 19 February 1916. To Longside from Kingsnorth by rail. First flight 16 June 1916. Exercised with Light Cruiser Squadron of the Grand Fleet, together with C.14, 7 October 1916. Crashed due to gas leak, car destroyed 29 January 1917. Deleted 3 January 1917, replaced.

C.5A

Reassembled Pembroke. Trials 27 August 1917. To Longside from Pembroke 24 March 1918. To East Fortune from Longside 29 October 1918. Deflated Howden 14 January 1919. Deleted October 1919. Hours flown 1917–18: 605 hours 14 minutes.

C.6

Built at Kingsnorth. Trials 27 August 1916. To Pembroke from Kingsnorth by rail 29 May 1916. Force landed at Germag, near Mullion 2 December 1916. Lost at sea returning from patrol due to engine trouble 23 March 1917. Deleted at Pembroke 24 March 1917, lost at sea.

C.7

Built at Kingsnorth. Trials 22 July 1916. To Longside from Kingsnorth by rail May 1916. Deflated in gale at Longside 21 September 1918. Deleted at Longside 1 October 1918, unserviceable. Hours flown: 123 hours August–December 1917, 649 hours 33 minutes 1918.

C.8

Built at Kingsnorth. Trials 16 May 1916. Took off from Kingsnorth 2 June 1916 on an endurance trial and when in vicinity of the Isle of Wight the engines broke down. Landed Polegate after being in the air for 14 hours 15 minutes. Only damage was a broken skid. To Kingsnorth 8 June 1916. Started to fly to Mullion, but, from some cause which was never discovered, the ship came down in the Channel. The captain, Flt Lt Dickinson, and two of the crew were drowned, only the W/T operator surviving. Deleted Kingsnorth 9 June 1916, lost at sea.

C.9

Built at Kingsnorth. To Mullion from Kingsnorth by rail 15 June 1916. Trials 1 July 1916. Free-balloon descent into sea 23 July 1916 after 19 hour flight covering 520 miles. Taken in tow by destroyer and disembarked with some damage to envelope and car.

C.5A landing. Note the 2-bladed propellers, air-scoop to the rear of the aft engine, and the aft engine radiator on the outboard of the car instead of above, as on the C.1. (Stuart Leslie)

C.7 in flight at Longside, 1918. (Ces Mowthorpe Collection)

C.8 landing at Kingsnorth, June 1916. Note that the engines are stopped. (JMB/GSL Collection)

Shared destruction of a U-boat with C.2 and C.23A and destroyer HMS *Laverock* in September 1917 (Flt Lt Struthers DSC). Another successful attack was carried out on 3 October 1917; oil and bubbles indicated a sunken U-boat but C.9 had to depart owing to shortage of fuel and a rising gale. She arrived back at Mullion 6 hours later with almost empty tanks. C.9. was taken over by Flt Lt T.P. York-Moore 17 December 1917. Hours flown: 177 hours 27 minutes 1916, 1,042 hours 42 minutes 1917, 1,280 hours 2 minutes 1918. C.9 flew approximately 68,201 miles, during a life of 805 days, averaging 3 hours 6 minutes flying time per day. Deflated for survey 14 September 1918. Deleted Mullion 1 October 1918, unserviceable.

C.10

Built at Kingsnorth. Trials 6 May 1916. To Mullion from Kingsnorth by rail 19 June 1916. First flight Mullion 6 August 1916. Deleted after accident at Mullion 10 October 1916, replaced.

C.10A

At Longside August–November 1917. Exercised with Grand Fleet 16 September 1917 (with C.14, C.18 and C.20 plus NS–1 and NS–3). Hours flown: 71 hours 1917, 273 hours 1918. Deleted Longside 17 July 1918, unserviceable.

C.11

Built at Kingsnorth. Trials 9 June 1916. To Howden from Kingsnorth 26 June 1916 (damaged propeller on landing). Wrecked at Scarborough 23 April 1917 (Capt Hogg-Turner) but no fatalities.

C.11A

Rebuilt at Howden. Burst into flames over Humber 21 July 1917; two officers, two coxswains and W/T operator killed. Deleted Kingsnorth 12 March 1918, replaced by C*2.

C.12

Built at Kingsnorth. Trials 19 June 1916. To Polegate from Kingsnorth 23 June 1916. To Kingsnorth from Polegate for refit 1 August 1916. Deleted Kingsnorth 12 March 1918. Replaced by C*1. The car of C.12 was modified and became C*1.

C.13 (14A)

Built at Kingsnorth. Trials 3 July 1916. Wrecked at Kingsnorth 14 July 1916 through defective valve. To Cranwell from Kingsnorth 22 January 1917. Deflated after breaking away from handling party 27 July 1917. Envelope sent to Pulham from Cranwell 15 October 1917. Car delivered to Pulham November 1917 and renumbered C.14A. Wrecked entering shed in storm 27 July 1917. To Howden from Pulham 23 November 1918. Hours flown 1918: 35 hours. No photograph of C.13 can be traced.

C.14

Built at Kingsnorth. Trials 20 July 1916. To Longside from Kingsnorth September 1916. On 7 October exercised with Light Cruiser Squadron of Grand Fleet with C.5. Exercised with Grand Fleet 16 September 1917 (with C.10A, C.18 and C.20 plus NS–1 and NS–3). Hours flown: 153 hours August–December 1917, 343 hours 15 minutes 1918. Deleted Longside 17 July 1918, unserviceable.

C.15

Built at Kingsnorth. Trials 26 July 1916. To East Fortune from Kingsnorth via Howden 23 August 1916. Carried out towing trials with HMS *Phaeton* from East Fortune on 3 May 1917. Further towing trials with HMS *Phaeton* on 5 June 1917. Deleted East Fortune 16 July 1917, wrecked while towing. No photograph of C.15 can be traced.

C.16

Built at Kingsnorth. Trials 7 August 1916. To East Fortune from Kingsnorth via Cranwell

C.9, Mullion, July 1916. Note the 'Coastal shed' being erected. The other 'Coastal' in flight is probably C.2. (JMB/GSL Collection)

C.10A taking off from Longside. (Ces Mowthorpe Collection)

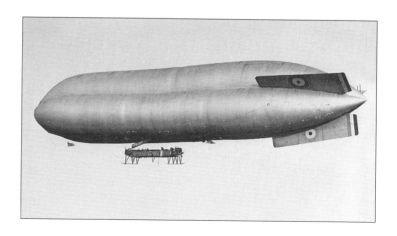

C.11 fitted with a Renault engine. (The Royal Aeronautical Society)

and Howden 23 August 1916. On 28 August 1916 both engines stopped over the sea due to magneto failure. Free-balloon descent was made into sea at north end of Coldingham Bay, near Berwick. Ship a total wreck but no lives lost. Deleted East Fortune 4 September 1916. 196 ft overall, 170,000 cu ft, one 150 hp Sunbeam (tractor), one 220 hp Renault (pusher). Armament as C.1.

C.17

Built at Kingsnorth. Trials 10 August 1916, captained by Flt Lt Wheelwright. To Pulham from Kingsnorth 31 August 1916. On 15 November 1916, while experimenting with a new type of grapnel, the trail rope fouled a propeller which shattered and pierced the envelope. On 13 February 1917 conducted experiments dropping parachutes. In April 1917 Col Maitland made a parachute descent from 1,000 ft. On 21 April 1917 proceeded on patrol, but no contact was made with base after 08.00 hours. Captain was Sub Lt E.G.O. Jackson, observer Assistant Paymaster R.A.P. Walters. Deleted Pulham 21 April 1917, destroyed by fire. It was assumed that C.17 had been shot down by German seaplanes. There were no survivors. Prior to this the Lewis gun on top of the envelope had not often been carried but, as a result of the loss of C.17, instructions were issued that the upper gun was to be manned whenever 'Coastals' were operated out of Pulham over the North Sea. Assistant Paymaster Walters had only gone on C.17 as a passenger for some air experience.

C.18

Built at Kingsnorth. Trials 22 August 1916. To Longside from Kingsnorth November 1916. Exercised with Grand Fleet 16 September 1917 (with C.10A, C.14 and C.20 plus NS–1 and NS–3). To East Fortune from Longside 16 April 1918 (damaged and deflated upon landing). To Longside from Kingsnorth 19 April 1918. Hours flown: 160 hours August–December 1917, 131 hours 22 minutes 1918. Deleted Kingsnorth 31 August 1918. Replaced by new type.

C.19

Built at Kingsnorth. Trials 31 August 1916. To Howden from Kingsnorth 11 September 1916. To Kingsnorth from Howden (last flight) 14 March 1918. Hours flown: 303 hours August–December 1917, 84 hours 40 minutes 1918. Deleted Kingsnorth 31 August 1918, replaced by new type. A 100 hp Green (tractor) was fitted at some stage.

C.20

Built at Kingsnorth. Trials 12 September 1916. To East Fortune from Kingsnorth 23 September 1916. Made the first airship flight with the Battle Cruiser Fleet, being ordered about visually during this experiment, 30 September 1916. Exercised with Grand Fleet 16 September 1917 (with C.10A, C.14, and C.18 plus NS–1 and NS–3). Made forced landing in sea, rammed by HMS *Criana*; sunk by gunfire 22 December 1917. Hours flown, 110 hours. Deleted East Fortune 22 December 1917, lost at sea.

C.21

Built at Kingsnorth. Trials 21 September 1916. To Howden from Kingsnorth 26 September 1916. To Folkestone from Howden 15 February 1918. On taking off from Folkestone 1 June 1918, forward handling guys hit roof of a hut and were flung upward, hitting and shattering forward propeller which pierced forward ballonet and envelope. During free-ballooning descent the car was wrecked beyond repair. Hours flown: 148 hours August–December 1917, 290 hours 3 minutes 1918. Deleted Folkestone 2 June 1918, unserviceable. A 100 hp Green (tractor) was fitted at some stage.

C.12, in 'A' shed at Polegate, 5 October 1916. SS–16 is in the background. Note the loose linen tube leading across the shed to the air-scoop. This kept pressure up in the ballonets via a portable compressor. (JMB/GSL Collection)

C.14, Longside, 1914. Note the early type of air-scoop, and the Lewis gun, mounted in the ready position. (JMB/GSL Collection)

The wreck of C.16 after both engines failed, Coldingham Bay, near Berwick, 28 August 1916. (Fleet Air Arm Museum; neg. no. A/SHIP/123A)

C.18 at Longside. The captain is climbing aboard. Note the Lewis gun in the stowed position. (JMB/GSL Collection)

C.17 leaving Pulham. (JMB/GSL Collection)

C.19 preparing for take off on a war patrol.
(The Royal Aeronautical Society)

C.20 landing at East Fortune. (Ces Mowthorpe
Collection)

C.22

Built at Kingsnorth. Trials 21 September 1916. Moved to Mullion October 1916. Lost in Channel midway between Lands End and Ushant in bad weather 21 March 1917 due to both engines failing. Crew of 'Long, Jones, Thurnbull and McCall' were all saved. Deleted 21 March 1917 at Mullion, lost at sea.

C.23

Built at Kingsnorth. Trials 16 October 1916. To Folkestone from Kingsnorth 24 October 1916. Airship collapsed and fell into field near station owing to upper Lewis gun striking envelope 1 May 1917. Deleted 11 May 1917, replaced.

C.23A

Trials at Folkestone 11 July 1917. To Mullion from Folkestone 4 September 1917. The senior flying officer at Mullion complained in April 1918 that 'HMA C.23A's envelope had been inflated for over 10 months and had done just under 1,000 hours flying and great difficulty was being experienced in handling this ship in bad weather'. Wrecked at sea off Newbury 10 May 1918. W/T operator drowned, the pilot, Capt A.S. Elliott, and the engineer were saved. Wreck towed into Newbury and salvaged. It was discovered that the after crab-pot had carried away, allowing the envelope to deflate. Hours flown: 424 hours at Mullion 1917, 475 hours 10 minutes 1918. Deleted Mullion 10 May 1918, wrecked at sea.

C.24

Built at Kingsnorth. Trials 23 October 1916. To East Fortune from Kingsnorth by rail. First flight 13 December 1916. Made flight of 24 hours 15 minutes from East Fortune 9/10 July 1917. Exercised with Grand Fleet 4 November 1917. Hours flown: 260 hours 59 minutes August–December 1917. Deleted Kingsnorth 4 April 1918, replaced by C*3. No photograph of this airship can be traced.

C.25

Built at Kingsnorth. Trials 26 October 1916. To East Fortune from Kingsnorth by rail. Accidentally deflated on ground 28 December 1917. Made balloon landing at Balmackie, near Dundee, due to engine trouble. Moored out and damaged by wind 1 February 1918. To Longside from East Fortune 29 July 1918. Last heard of while on patrol at 18.40 hours on 31 July 1918, 60 miles east of Aberdeen; Capt Hopperton and crew lost; a propeller belonging to C.25 was found at this position. C.25 was searching for a reputedly damaged U-boat, together with several other 'Coastals'. It was generally believed that C.25 came upon the U-boat, which was unable to dive and so engaged C.25 with her deck gun, scoring a direct hit. Confirmation was sought from German records after the war but it was discovered that the U-boat in question never returned to base after that patrol. Hours flown: 66 hours November–December 1917, 650 hours 6 minutes 1918. Deleted Longside 31 July 1918, lost at sea. A 100 hp Green (tractor) was fitted at some stage.

C.26

Built at Kingsnorth. Trials 8 November 1916. To Pulham from Kingsnorth 21 November 1916. Forced landing 3 miles from Howden due to petrol shortage 1 October 1917. Deflated and returned to Pulham. On 12 December 1917, C.26's captain, Flt Lt Kilburn, a close friend of C.27's Fl Lt Dixon who had gone missing the day before, begged his CO to allow him to go out and search for C.27 and her missing crew. Despite marginal weather conditions this request was granted and C.26 departed. Desperately searching for signs of C.27, Flt Lt Kilburn stretched his airship's endurance to the limit. Unfortunately, with a rising head-wind, he

C.21 on patrol. (Ces Mowthorpe Collection)

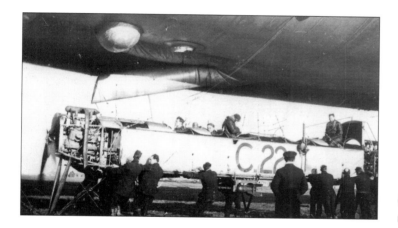

C.22 ready for flight. (Fleet Air Arm Museum; neg. no. A/SHIP/364)

C.23A landing at Mullion, 1917. (JMB/GSL Collection)

C.25, a front view of the modified car, East Fortune, 1917. (The Royal Aeronautical Society)

C.25 with the modified covered car. East Fortune, 1918. (The Royal Aeronautical Society)

C.26 landing. (Ces Mowthorpe Collection)

C.27 executing a forced landing. Note that the engines are stopped and the triangular 'forced landing' pennant is being flown below the bows. The ship is valving gas and gently descending into the hands of the emergency handling party, prior to being walked across the fields back to Pulham. (Ces Mowthorpe Collection)

ran out of fuel and drifted over Holland; landed at Portugal near Dordrecht, Holland, with crew. Ship broke away and landed further north at Eesmes, near the Zuyder Zee. Flt Lts Kilburn and Plowden and crew were interned. Hours flown: 202 hours August–December 1917. Deleted Pulham 13 December 1917, force landed Holland.

C.27
Built at Kingsnorth. Trials 13 December 1916. To Pulham from Kingsnorth 16 December 1916. (captained by Flt Lts Barton and Godfrey). On 13 February 1917 Col Maitland's parachute descent was filmed from C.17 in cine and still. Reported to Pulham as being seen to fall into sea in flames on 11 December 1917, presumably the result of an attack by German seaplanes. Flt Lts Dixon and Hall perished with crew. Hours flown: 314 hours August–December 1917. Deleted Pulham 11 December 1917, destroyed by fire.

No photographs of the following airships sold abroad can be traced.

'COASTALS' A, B, C, D, E

'Coastals' A, B, C and D were sold to the Russian Government. They were tested at Kingsnorth and departed England on 3 July 1916. They were delivered by sea to Sebastopol, arriving 17 October 1916. Originally named *Albatros*, *Chaika*, *Delfin* and *Chernomor*, they operated only with Fleet Tactical Numbers 1, 2, 3 and 4. Two Russian naval officers came to Kingsnorth in order to train in flying and handling 'Coastals'. Two RN officers, Flt Lt Shanks and Lt H.K. Hitchcock RNVR, went to Russia with the ships to assemble them and instruct new crews. No. 1 made its first flight in Russia on 11 December 1916. On 16 December 1916 she force landed in sea due to

engine failure and never flew again. No. 2 (renamed *Kondor*) was destroyed by fire in her hangar on 27 March 1917. The other two 'Coastals' do not appear to have been assembled. 'Coastal' E was sold to the French Government, sailing on 23 August 1916 (see C.4, p. 48).

THE 'COASTAL STAR' CLASS (C*)

The 'Coastal Star' ('C*') class was developed because of problems which beset the new 'North Sea' class in 1917 (see p. xx). It was an interim type produced at short notice by the development team at RNAS Kingsnorth. Although closely related to the 'Coastals' – the C*1 prototype was a modified C.12 – the 'Coastal Stars' had a number of significant differences.

The envelope was a completely new design. Still of tri-lobe section, it was quite streamlined and increased to 207 ft in length, with a capacity of 210,000 cu ft. To improve stability, six ballonets were fitted, all connected to a main duct leading to the air-scoop which collected air from the slipstream of the after propeller. In the first 'Coastal Stars', this duct was external, but it was fitted internally to later ships in order to reduce drag. After the first three 'C*' airships, which had a rather blunt tail cone, the envelope was lengthened by 10 ft without alteration to the capacity. The result was a much 'finer' and pleasing shape.

Although the open cockpits were retained, the car was covered with plywood instead of canvas, and now incorporated four circular glass 'portholes' on either side and a glass panel in the floor. The engine mounts were extended, and several other modifications improved the crew comfort.

Originally the engines were a 220 hp Renault aft and a 110 hp Berliet forward. The Renault was sometimes replaced by a 240 hp Fiat. A small engine in the car powered the generator with means of activating a blower to maintain ballonet pressure if required. Fuel was in cylindrical tanks suspended from canvas bridles attached to the suspension system inside the envelope.

Usually four 85 gal tanks were fitted. The gunner's position on top of the envelope was omitted, but Lewis guns were carried in the car. Racks for two 230 lb and two 100 lb bombs were carried. For the first time provision was made for parachutes, carried externally on lines that could be attached quickly to the harnesses worn by all five crew members.

The original order for twenty 'Coastal Stars' was cut back to ten in July 1918 in favour of the 'SS-Twin' design which had several advantages over the 'Coastal Star' ships.

All ten 'Coastal Stars' had successful operational careers and were the subject of two novel schemes, neither of which were implemented. The first was to fit these airships with two 'circling-torpedoes' with shallow depth settings, for attacking U-boats at periscope depth. The second was to use them as air ambulances, escorted by fighter planes, for moving urgent surgery cases to British hospitals from the Western Front.

THE 'COASTAL STAR' SHIPS

Length: 207 ft (C*1–C*3), 217 ft rest
Width: 49 ft 3 in
Capacity: 210,000 cu ft
Engines: 240 hp Fiat and 110 hp Berliet-Ford, both water-cooled

C*1

Built at Kingsnorth. Trials 30 January 1918. To East Fortune from Kingsnorth via Howden and Pulham 17 February 1918. Deflated January 1919, deleted October 1919. Hours flown 1918: 868 hours 7 minutes.

C*2

Built at Kingsnorth. Trials 9 March 1918. To Howden from Kingsnorth via Pulham 14 March 1918. Deflated January 1919. Deleted October 1919. Hours flown 1918: 560 hours 40 minutes.

C*3

Built at Kingsnorth. Trials 30 March 1918. To East Fortune via Cranwell and Howden 4 April 1918. Deflated January 1919. Deleted October 1919. Hours flown 1918: 588 hours 7 minutes.

C*4

Built at Kingsnorth. Trials 5 May 1918. To Howden from Kingsnorth via Pulham 8 May 1918. Made a recorded flight of 34 hours 30 minutes on 27/28 May 1918 (Capt Cleary). To Longside from Howden via East Fortune 16 November 1918. Deflated January 1919. Deleted October 1919. Hours flown 1918: 509 hours 23 minutes.

C*5

Built at Kingsnorth. Trials 15 May 1918. To Longside from Kingsnorth via Pulham and Howden 19 May 1918. Forced landing through engine trouble 2 June 1918. Capts McColl and Underhill. Deflated January 1919. Deleted October 1919. Hours flown 1918: 536 hours 56 minutes.

C*6

Built at Kingsnorth. Trials 25 May 1918. To Mullion from Kingsnorth 29 May 1918. Deflated 26 July 1918. Dispatched by rail to Kingsnorth for repairs 20 August 1918. To Mullion from Kingsnorth 11 October 1918. To Pulham from Kingsnorth 3 January 1919. Deflated 27 May 1919. Hours flown: 520 hours 20 minutes 1918, 2 hours 30 minutes 1919. Capts Montague, May and Booth.

C*1 on trials at Kingsnorth, 30 January 1918.
(Ces Mowthorpe Collection)

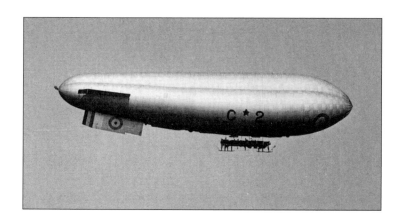

C*2 over Howden, 1 June 1918. (The Royal
Aeronautical Society)

C*3 in flight over East Fortune. (JMB/GSL
Collection)

C*4, based at Howden, East Fortune and Longside.
(Fleet Air Arm Museum; neg. no. A/SHIP/353)

C*5 taking off from Longside. Note the handing crew below. This was the minimum number required to move a 'Coastal' in calm conditions. In higher winds, double the number were required. (JMB/GSL Collection)

C*10 landing at Mullion. Note the tail section is more streamlined (thinner) than early 'Coastal *s'. (JMB/GSL Collection)

C*6 at 400 ft off the Cornish coast, 5 June 1918. (Fleet Air Arm Museum; neg. no. A/SHIP/361)

C*7 landing at Longside, 13 October 1918. C*5 is in the background. (JMB/GSL Collection)

C*8 in the shed, possibly at East Fortune. Note that the car is 'decorated overall', as if being used as a rostrum. Perhaps the photograph was taken during Armistice celebrations. (JMB/GSL Collection)

C*9 preparing for flight at Howden. (Fleet Air Arm Museum; neg. no. A/SHIP/354)

C*7
Built at Kingsnorth. Trials 8 June 1918. To East Fortune from Kingsnorth via Pulham and Cranwell 17 June 1918. To Longside from East Fortune 31 September 1918. Deflated Longside 2 November 1918. Deflated January 1919. Deleted October 1919. Hours flown 1918: 330 hours 40 minutes.

C*8

Built at Kingsnorth. Trials 17 June 1918. To Cranwell from Kingsnorth 6 July 1918. To East Fortune from Cranwell 11 August 1918. Deflated 25 January 1919. Hours flown 1918: 204 hours 13 minutes.

C*9
Built at Kingsnorth. Trials 28 June 1918. To Howden from Kingsnorth via Pulham 29 July 1918. Damaged by bomb exploding on landing ground 24 September 1918 (last flight). Deflated Howden January 1919. Hours flown 1918: 163 hours 57 minutes.

C*10
Built at Kingsnorth. Trials 6 July 1918. Mullion from Kingsnorth 29 July 1918. Kingsnorth from Toller (Mullion) 8 November 1918. Deleted October 1919. Hours flown in 1918: 655 hours 50 minutes. Length 217 ft, width 49 ft 3 in, volume 210,000 cu ft. Engines 360 hp Fiat and 110 hp Berliet-Ford, both water-cooled.

CHAPTER 5

THE 'NORTH SEAS'

THE 'NORTH SEA' CLASS

This class of large non-rigids was introduced in 1917 as a stop-gap for use with the Fleet until large rigid airships came into service. At first the 'North Seas' were plagued with drive-shaft troubles. These were so serious that a halt was called to production after the first five were completed, bringing about the hybrid 'Coastal Star' class to fill the gap.

Thankfully, by 1918 the expertise of the Royal Navy's airshipmen had solved the problem. Subsequently, the fifteen 'North Sea' airships proved to be perhaps the finest non-rigids in the world, establishing a supremacy amongst non-rigid lighter-than-air craft which culminated in the interwar American Goodyear 'blimps'.

The specification for the new airships, approved in January 1916, was for an envelope of 360,000 cu ft capacity, 262 ft long, containing six ballonets with a total capacity of 128,000 cu ft. It would be powered by two Rolls-Royce 250 hp Eagle engines, giving an endurance of 20 hours at a maximum of 55 m.p.h. With subsequent modifications speeds up to 70 m.p.h. were occasionally attained.

NS–1, the first of the class, carried out her trials flight on 1 February 1917 at RNAS Kingsnorth were she had been designed and built.

The envelope was a (by now) typical tri-lobe Astra-Torres type, but of streamline shape. Fuel tanks were originally fitted externally to the envelope as on other Naval non-rigids, but the longer fuel-lines necessary were prone to fracturing with the movement between envelope and engines, so they were subsequently re-hung on special 'straps' internally – directly above the control car. A canvas tube through the envelope led to an observation/gun platform on the top. Access to this tube was by open ladder from the control car. Two vertical fins were attached to the stern in the now normal manner. A rudder was affixed to the bottom fin only. Horizontal tailplanes and elevators were fitted to the lower lobes, similar to other Naval non-rigids.

The completely enclosed control car, 35 ft long with 6 ft headroom, was constructed of steel tubes, covered with duralumin sheets and fabric. This contained (from front to back) a spacious control room with a navigation room with W/T 'shack' opposite. Further aft still was the living and sleeping accommodation. With a crew of ten – two watches of five – it was possible to carry out extended patrols lasting several days. Provision for cooking was a hot-plate specially fitted to an engine exhaust.

Astern of the tapered control car, and connected to it by a walkway on steel cables, was the small engine car. This had space for two engineers plus their engine controls. Communication between the cars was by ship-type engine telegraphs.

In the first Admiralty design the two engines were mounted on either side of the engine car on a common platform. However, because of the complicated drive-shafts from the engines to the propellers, a number of variations to the position of the engine car and platform were tried. The situation was eased somewhat by replacing the Rolls-Royce engines with direct-drive Fiats. Finally, a complete redesign at East Fortune (under the supervision of Capt Wheelwright and Station Engineering Officer Lt Cdr A.S. Abell) successfully combined the two separate cars into one long car: the engines were still outboard, but they now drove the propellers direct.

Approved by the Admiralty, this arrangement became known as the Wheelwright design, and other 'North Sea' ships were similarly modified, notably NS–4. Meanwhile the Kingsnorth design team had found its own solution. This was similar in many ways to the Wheelwright type, but retained two separate cars. During late 1918, a further engine change took place, Rolls-Royce Eagle VIIIs replacing the Fiat engines on several ships.

Like the 'Coastals', the North Seas were armed. Up to five machine-guns could be fitted, but three was the norm: one on the upper platform and one mounted each side through the control car windows. Up to six 230 lb bombs were carried.

THE 'NORTH SEA' SHIPS

Builder: RNAS Kingsnorth
Length: 260 ft
Height: 69 ft
Diameter: 57 ft
Capacity: 360,000 cu ft
Ballonet capacity (6): 128,000 cu ft
Top speed: 57 m.p.h.
Endurance: 24 hours
Engines: Two 250 hp Rolls-Royce Eagle engines originally, later replaced by 240 hp Fiats
Gross lift: 10.85 tons
Disposable lift: 3.8 tons

NS–1

Trials flight Kingsnorth 2 February 1917. To Pulham from Kingsnorth 8 April 1917 (captained by Lt Cdr Robinson). Flight of 49 hours 22 minutes (1,536 miles) on 26/27 June 1917. To Kingsnorth from Pulham for repairs 17 July 1917. To East Fortune via Pulham 6 September 1917. From East Fortune to Longside September 1917. At Longside October 1917. At East Fortune November/December 1917. Force landed at Fenwick, south of Berwick, on 11 December 1917. Hours flown 1917: 206 hours 57 minutes. Deleted Kingsnorth 22 February 1918, replaced.

NS–2

Trials flight Kingsnorth 16 June 1917. Wrecked at Stonham, 4 miles east of Stowmarket, 27 June 1917. Deleted Kingsnorth 22 February 1918, replaced.

NS–3

To East Fortune from Kingsnorth 22 July 1917. Landed at Longside with engine trouble 10 December 1917. Returned to East Fortune 21 December 1917. Flt Cdr J.S. Wheelwright and Lt Cdr A.S. Abell officially reconstructed the enclosed car, the Rolls-Royce engines being replaced by 240 hp Fiats. The car was then slung closer beneath the envelope (NS–4 was likewise modified). Trials 11, 12 March 1918, made night flight over Fleet at Rosyth. Attained a record height of 10,000 ft on 31 May 1918. Towed at 30 knots behind HMS *Vectis* 18 June 1918. Landed on water alongside HMS *Vectis* and changed crews by whaler 19 June 1918. On patrol 21 June 1918 when sighted oil-slick and took part in attack with a destroyer. Later, returning to base in the early hours of 22 June, was wrecked off Dunbar in high gale (Capts Wheelwright and P.E. Maitland both rescued, but five crew drowned). Hours flown: 323 hours 48 minutes 1917, 323 hours 4 minutes 1918. Deleted 22 June 1918.

NS–4

Trials Kingsnorth 17 September 1917. To East Fortune from Kingsnorth 15 October

NS–1 on her trial flight at Kingsnorth, 2 February 1917. Note the absence of markings and the original disposition of the fuel tanks, engines and cars. (Ces Mowthorpe Collection)

NS–3 during her trials flight at East Fortune, 12 March 1918, after being modified to 'Wheelwright' design. (Ces Mowthorpe Collection)

NS–4 at Howden, October 1918. The car is the East Fortune modification known as the 'Wheelwright' design. (JMB/GSL Collection)

NS-2 wrecked at Stoneham, near Stowmarket, 27 June 1917. (Fleet Air Arm Museum; neg. no. A/SHIP/368)

1917. To Longside from East Fortune 17 June 1918. To East Fortune from Longside 27 August 1918. To Kingsnorth from East Fortune 29 August 1918. To Howden from Kingsnorth via Cranwell 13 October 1918. To Longside from Cranwell via Howden 23 October 1918 (Capt W.K. Warneford). Hours flown: 104 hours 39 minutes 1917, 160 hours 50 minutes 1918. Deflated Longside 6 February 1919. Deleted October 1919.

NS–5

Trials Kingsnorth 18 November 1917. Allocated to East Fortune. To Howden from Kingsnorth 12 December 1917. To East Fortune from Howden 12 December 1918. Made forced landing at Ayton through engine trouble in high wind; envelope wrecked on trees. Ship was en route to East Fortune from Kingsnorth. Deleted 22 February 1918 Kingsnorth, replaced.

NS–6

First flight January 1918. Acceptance trials 21/22 May 1918. To Longside from Kingsnorth via East Fortune 31 May 1918. Remained at Longside until deflated 8 February 1919. Commanded mostly by Capt Struthers but by Capt Montague on 17/18 November 1918. Hours flown 1918: 397 hours 35 minutes. Deleted October 1919.

NS–7

Acceptance trials 6/7 June 1918. To East Fortune from Kingsnorth via Pulham 29 June 1918. When the German Fleet surrendered and sailed into British waters, NS–7 was in position on the starboard bow. To Howden from East Fortune February 1920. From Howden to Pulham and return 3 March 1920. Instructing American crew training to take over R.38 on 3 and 8 June 1920, and on 9 and 21 September 1920. Hours flown: 204 hours 33 minutes 1918, approximately 247 hours 1919/20. The last non-rigid to serve

with the RAF. Final flight 25 October 1921. Deleted October 1921.

NS–8

First flight 29 June 1918. Acceptance trials 1 and 4 July 1918. To East Fortune from Kingsnorth 29 July 1918. Forced landing at Johnshaven 5 August 1918. Capt Chambers and Capt Cleary. When the German Fleet surrendered and sailed into British waters, NS–8 was in position over the centre of the Fleet. To Howden 1919. Hours flown: 222 hours 29 minutes 1918, 58 hours 1919.

NS–9

First flight 28 July 1918. Acceptance trials 29 July 1918. To Longside from Kingsnorth 31 July 1918. First patrol (16 hours) on 1 August 1918. Shot at by enemy U-boat in mist (Capt P.E. Maitland). 'Ripped' when caught in gale at Longside 21 September 1918. Kingsnorth for repairs 14 September 1918. Hours flown 1918: 151 hours 40 minutes. Deleted 3 October 1918 Longside, replaced.

NS–10

To Longside from Kingsnorth via Howden 13 August 1918. Caught in gale and 'ripped' on return to Longside from patrol on 21 September 1918 (Capt Montague). Hours flown 1918: 128 hours 4 minutes. Deleted Longside 3 October 1918, replaced.

NS–11

To Longside from Kingsnorth via Howden 7 September 1918. Established world endurance record 9–13 February 1919 when she flew 4,000 miles in 100 hours 15 minutes on mine-hunting patrol. To East Fortune from Longside 5 March 1919. In company with NS–12 she made the first airship flight to Norway (24 hours) cruising off the Norwegian coast for several hours. To Cranwell from East Fortune via Howden,

NS—5 at Kingsnorth, December 1917. This photograph clearly shows the long propeller shafts of the early NS-ships, which gave such a lot of trouble until suitably modified at both East Fortune and Kingsnorth. (Ces Mowthorpe Collection)

NS—6 taking off. (Ces Mowthorpe Collection)

NS—7 being walked into her shed at East Fortune, summer 1918. (JMB/GSL Collection)

NS–8 preparing for flight, East Fortune, 1918. This was a 'Kingsnorth' modification. (Ces Mowthorpe Collection)

NS–9, Longside. Note the 'Admiralty'-type conversion, carried out at Kingsnorth, which can be compared with the 'Wheelwright' conversion done on the NS–4 at East Fortune. (JMB/GSL Collection)

NS–10 at Longside, 21 September 1918. Together with three other ships, NS–10 was recalled because of a rising gale. Wind gusts of up to 50 m.p.h. made a landing impossible so all four flew to the lee of the sheds and 'ripped' at 100 ft. Note the triangular ripping panel coming away from the bows. Fortunately, there were no casualties. NS–10 was never re-assembled because of the Armistice. (JMB/GSL Collection)

NS—11, Longside. (JMB/GSL Collection)

NS—13 during her trials at Kingsnorth, November 1918. She was later sold to the USA as NS—14. (The Royal Aeronautical Society)

NS—16 in flight. (JMB/GSL Collection)

Pulham and Kingsnorth 31 March 1919. To Pulham from Cranwell June 1919. Lost at sea 15 July 1919 (Capt W. Warneford), believed struck by lightning near Blakeney, Norfolk. Total hours flown: 228 hours 56 minutes 1918, 263 hours 1919.

NS–12

Trials flight 16 October 1918. Kingsnorth to Howden on 22 October. From Howden to East Fortune 23 October. From East Fortune to Longside 26 October 1918 (Capt P.E. Maitland). First patrol 29 October 1918. Made flight of 43 hours 25 minutes during 17 and 19 November 1918. Made 24 hour flight to Norway in company with NS–11 – first airship flight to Norway. Hours flown: 95 hours 24 minutes. Deleted 12 February 1919.

NS–13

Renumbered NS–14 and purchased by USA

on 8 November 1918. As NS–13 this ship made at least one flight, of 4 hours 50 minutes, under Capt Wheelwright, accompanied by Capt Yorke-Moore (source: B.G. Turpin).

NS–16

Accepted 10 January 1919. Took part in experiments to sweep mines by means of a airship-towed sweep. To Pulham from Kingsnorth 14 March 1919. Made 4 hour flight 15 March – returned to Pulham. To Howden from Pulham 23 March 1919 (Capt Montague). Deflated Howden 16 June 1919 owing to bad gas purity. Hours flown 1919: 89 hours 35 minutes.

NS–15, NS–17 AND NS–18

These airships were under construction and completed but never delivered or flown due to the Armistice.

NS–12, trials flight at Kingsnorth, 17 October 1918. (The Royal Aeronautical Society)

CHAPTER 6

THE 'SSPS' AND 'SSZS' (ZEROS)

THE 'SSP' CLASS

The year 1916 saw the RNAS looking for an airship which would take over from the original 'SS' ships, but with a better performance, thus easing the load on the 'Coastals'. Kingsnorth produced the first design, the 'SSP' – the Sea Scout Pusher.

As the most successful of the 'SS' ships were the ones that used a Maurice Farman aircraft fuselage, Kingsnorth decided to develop the rear-engined pusher format. Therefore it built a specially-designed car, far more spacious and comfortable than the Maurice Farman, to carry a crew of three, a pilot, W/T operator and engineer. This was rigged to one of the 70,000 cu ft envelopes which the later 'SS' ships used. Originally fitted with the new 75 hp Rolls-Royce Hawk engine, which was still suffering from teething troubles, it was later given the then more reliable 100 hp Green.

The result was a much longer car, with the air-scoop for the ballonets fitted right aft in the slipstream of the pusher engine. Consequently it became necessary to add an extra fin, forward of the normal lower fin and rudder to counteract the extra side area. Petrol tanks were slung either side of the envelope in what was becoming standard procedure for RNAS non-rigids.

The 'SSPs' started to come off the production line in spring 1917. However, only six were built. Three – Nos. 1, 5 and 6 – gave reasonable service until the Armistice. Unfortunately No. 2 was lost at sea on operations, as was No. 4, while No. 3 was wrecked on her delivery flight. The cost of an SSP was approximately £4,000.

THE 'SSP' SHIPS

Length: 143 ft
Diameter: 30 ft
Capacity: 70,000 cu ft

SSP–1
Built at Kingsnorth. Trials 31 January 1917, attained 52 m.p.h. To Folkestone from Kingsnorth 15 March 1917. To Kingsnorth from Folkestone 15 June 1917. To Anglesey from Kingsnorth 5 July 1917. To Cranwell from Anglesey via Howden 26 May 1918. Deflated Cranwell 28 January 1919. Deleted September 1919. Engine either 100 hp Green or 75 hp Rolls-Royce, both water-cooled.

SSP.2
Car built Wormwood Scrubs, assembled Kingsnorth. To Caldale from Kingsnorth via Howden 28 May 1917. Escorted 3rd Battlecruiser Squadron into harbour for 80 miles 3 November 1917. Lost at sea through engine trouble, northeast of Westry, on 26 November 1917. Flt Lt E.B. Devereux lost. Deleted Caldale 26 November 1917. Engine 100 hp Green, water-cooled. It appears probable that SSP.2 was assembled originally at Wormwood Scrubs, then flown to Kingsnorth in company with SSP.4. At Kingsnorth it was fitted with Remy ignition gear and a black envelope for its intended use with the BEF. Hence the delay in its 'first' flight in May (source: B.G. Turpin). (See also SSP.5.)

SSP.1 flying over the airfield at Barrow. (Ces Mowthorpe Collection)

SSP.2 taking off from Kingsnorth, May 1917.
(JMB/GSL Collection)

SSP.3 car under construction, Wormwood Scrubs,
January 1917. (The Royal Aeronautical Society)

SSP.4 preparing to take off from Caldale, 1917.
(Ces Mowthorpe Collection)

SSP.5 taking off from Barrow. (Ces Mowthorpe Collection)

SSP.6 being made ready at Wormwood Scrubs for her flight to Anglesey, via Cranwell and Howden, June 1917. Flt Sub Lt T.B. Williams (capt) is standing second from left. (T.B. Williams/Ces Mowthorpe Collection)

SSP.3

Built at Wormwood Scrubs. Trials 23 February 1917. To Folkestone from Wormwood Scrubs. Wrecked at Faversham en route 16 March 1917. Deleted Folkestone 21 March 1917, 'lost near Faversham'. Engine 100 hp Green, water-cooled.

SSP.4

Built at Wormwood Scrubs. To Caldale from Wormwood Scrubs via Howden 12 June 1917. Lost at sea in heavy snowstorm 21 December 1917. Flt Cdr Horner (Co) lost (see pp. 12 and 13 CB/819). Hours flown 1917: 165 hours. Deleted Caldale 22 December 1917, lost at sea. Engine 100 hp Green, water-cooled.

SSP.5

Built at Wormwood Scrubs. Originally modified to take a black envelope (85,000 cu ft) and fitted with silenced engine for secret night flights in France. Project cancelled. (See also SSP.2.) Some confusion exists about which of the two 'SSPs' was actually modified. To Anglesey from Wormwood Scrubs 18 January 1917. To Cranwell from Anglesey via Howden 26 March 1918. Hours flown 1917 and 1918: 370 hours. Deflated Cranwell 29 January 1919. Deleted Cranwell September 1919. Engine either 100 hp Green or 75 hp Rolls-Royce, both water-cooled.

SSP.6

Built at Wormwood Scrubs. Captained by T.B. Williams who took command 8 June 1917. To Anglesey from Wormwood Scrubs 16 June 1917. Abandoned in sea (engine trouble). Airship eventually 'landed' near Chichester 16 March 1918. To Cranwell from Anglesey 12 April 1918 (Capt G.E. Bungey). (Forced landing near Blackburn, Lancashire, and badly damaged.) Hours flown 1917 and 1918: 320 hours. Deleted

Cranwell September 1919. Engine 100 hp Green, water-cooled.

THE 'SSZ' CLASS

The reason for the limited production of 'SSPs' was because of the development of the 'SSZ' or 'Zero' at Capel. Not only was the car of superior design, the 'Zero' was powered with the now superb Rolls-Royce 75 hp Hawk, specially designed to power non-rigid airships.

The search for a successor for the original 'SS' ships had also been taken up by the engineering section at RNAS Capel, near Folkestone. Under Cdr A.D. Cunningham – a pioneer airshipman – every effort was made to improve operational capability. Particularly influential were the engineering officer, Lt F.M. Rope, and his chief artificer, WO Righton. Between them they designed and built a trim, streamlined boat-shaped car. This was an aluminium-covered ash frame, which, apart from the three cockpit openings, was watertight. This enabled the airship to land on calm water. The 'vee' bottom was specially strengthened so that normal landings could be carried out without the need of skids or 'bumping-bags'. The 'SSZ' car bore a superficial resemblance to that of the *Beta II* of 1913–14, with which the Capel team was familiar.

Equally innovative was the 75 hp Rolls-Royce water-cooled engine, the only engine ever to be designed specially for non-rigid airships. Reputedly, Lt Cave-Browne-Cave, the engineering officer at RNAS Kingsnorth, had complained bitterly about the adapted aeroplane engines, which, because of their unsuitability for slow flight, were giving endless trouble. In typical Naval fashion his CO told him to 'Get out and get a proper engine made'.

Taking him at his word, Lt Cave-Browne-Cave took a train to Derby and requested a meeting with Henry Royce. After two hours spent explaining his requirements, Lt Cave-Brown-Cave was sent back to Kingsnorth with the assurance that, if the Admiralty approved, Rolls-Royce would supply such an engine. The 75 hp Hawk was the result. It was, in the words of a well-known pilot, 'The sweetest engine ever run – it only stops when switched off or out of petrol'. This powerplant gave the 'SSZs' a maximum speed of 53 m.p.h. and a climb rate 1,200 ft per second.

The forward cockpit contained the W/T Operator surrounded by his equipment. He also had a machine-gun, which could be slung either side of his cockpit. This was not so much a practical defence as a useful tool for detonating floating mines. The pilot occupied the centre seat together with his instruments and toggles.

Aft was the engineer who had a starting handle which enabled him to hand-start the engine – and, because it was also geared to the auxiliary air-pump, which would enable pressure to be maintained in the ballonets if the engine failed. Two 110 lb bombs (or one 250 lb bomb) were carried either side just forward of the engine. An aerial camera could be carried but was rarely fitted.

All of this was attached to a 70,000 cu ft envelope with its two ballonets, both supplied with air from an air-scoop. Petrol was carried by the now usual aluminium cylindrical tanks, slung either side of the envelope. Various combinations of tanks – two, four or six – were used. The tail surfaces were almost identical with those of the later 'SS' ships, i.e. horizontal fins and elevators combined with a single, larger vertical fin with rudder.

In its original form, the after engineer's cockpit was fully enclosed, with a large opening window on either side. This was to give the engineer some protection from the noise and vibration of the engine, above

and behind him. Ground runs before it flew proved this idea impractical, so it was discarded, together with the fairing around the struts supporting the engine-bearers.

After it had completed its trials in September 1916, the Admiralty was informed of the prototype's success. Wheels were therefore set in motion to mass-produce the new airship, but not before Cdr Cunningham and his team were strongly rebuked for 'making unauthorised modifications to Naval equipment'!

At Capel, the prototype was initially designated the SS.0, which was spoken 'SS-Zero'. This in turn was inscribed on the car as SS.Z1. Deflated in April 1917, the SS.Z1 was sent to Messrs Frederick Sage & Co, at Peterborough, to serve as a pattern for production ships. Upon her return in August 1917 she was redesignated SSZ.1. The cost of a 'Zero' was approximately £5,000.

THE 'SSZ' SHIPS

Length: 143 ft
Diameter: 32 ft
Volume: 70,000 cu ft
Engine: Rolls-Royce Hawk 75 hp engine

SSZ.1
Built at Folkestone (between June and August). This prototype first flew without any markings, then it was marked SS.Z1. Trials 2 September 1916. Marked thus, on 5 April 1917 it was sent to Messrs Sage & Co, Furniture Manufacturers, as a pattern for the company to mass-produce the basic 'SSZ' car. Arrived back at Kingsnorth 21 August 1917. Ship inflated at Kingsnorth and renumbered SSZ.1. First flight 9 September 1917. Flew from Folkestone 1916–18. On 16 September 1918, piloted by Ensign N.J. Learned (American Navy), sighted oil-slick from U-boat. Called patrol boats on W/T and they depth-charged until the submarine, UB–103,

was destroyed. Hours flown: 960 hours. Deflated 14 January 1919. Deleted October 1919.

SSZ.2

Built at Folkestone. Trials 4 June 1917. Escorting transports to Boulogne, developed engine trouble and drifted across funnels of assisting destroyer, bursting into flames. Deleted Folkestone 14 August 1917, lost at sea. No photograph of SSZ.2 has been traced.

SSZ.3

Built at Folkestone. Trials 12 June 1917. To Pulham from Folkestone 12 December 1917. Took part in trials of a single-wire mooring system using a winch truck. To East Fortune from Pulham via Howden 17 July 1918. Towing trial with submarine K.5 on 3 August 1918. Hours flown 1917–18: 268 hours. Deleted East Fortune 7 December 1918.

SSZ.4

Built at Folkestone. Trials 25 June 1917. Served at Folkestone throughout. Hours flown: 193 hours 35 minutes 1917, 1,006 hours 26 minutes 1918. Deflated Folkestone 24 December 1918. Deleted Folkestone October 1919.

SSZ.5

Built at Folkestone. Trials 12 July 1917. Served at Folkestone. Destroyed by fire at Godmersham Park 17 September 1918. Hours flown: 254 hours 1917, 1,011 hours 35 minutes 1918. Deleted Folkestone 17 September 1918, 'destroyed by fire at Godmersham Park'.

SSZ.6

Assembled at Polegate. Trials 5 July 1917. Served at Polegate. Hours flown: 280 hours 1917, 753 hours 1918. Deflated 12 December 1918. Deleted Polegate October 1919.

SSZ.7

Assembled at Polegate. Trials 10 July 1917. Landed in fog on 20 December 1917 and collided with SSZ.10. Both destroyed by fire. Flt Sub Lt Swallow killed. Deleted Polegate 20 December 1917, destroyed by fire. Hours flown 1917: 376 hours.

SSZ.8

Assembled at Polegate. Trials 13 July 1917. Served at Polegate. Hours flown: 389 hours 1917, 825 hours 1918. Deflated 10 December 1918. Deleted Polegate October 1919. No photograph of SSZ–8 can be traced.

SSZ.9

Assembled at Polegate. Trials 27 July 1917. Served at Polegate. Made forced landing near Berthouville, south of Rouen, France, on 24 August 1918, pilot Lt Morlebury. Hours flown: 240 hours 1917, 786 hours 1918. Deleted Polegate 22 January 1919.

SSZ.10

Assembled at Polegate. Trials 4 August 1917. Served at Polegate. Landed in fog and collided with SSZ.7 20 December 1917; Flt Lt Watson injured. Deleted Polegate 20 December 1917, destroyed by fire. Hours flown 1917: 320 hours. No photograph of SSZ.10 can be traced.

SSZ.11

Assembled at Luce Bay. Trials 21 July 1917. Served at Luce Bay. Hours flown: 203 hours 1917, 1,406 hours 1918. Deflated 31 December 1918. Deleted Luce Bay October 1919. No photograph of SSZ.11 can be traced.

SSZ.12

Assembled at Luce Bay. Trials 17 July 1917. Served at Luce Bay. Collided with flagstaff on Stranraer pier, deflated and damaged 15 July

A prototype SSZ-car, fitted with the enclosed engineer's position. Designed to offer some protection, it defeated its purposes because of the horrendous noise and vibration that occurred within the confined space. This semi-enclosed 'Zero' never flew. It was eventually converted back to normal. (Ces Mowthorpe Collection)

SSZ.1 (prototype 'Zero') preparing for her trials flight at Folkestone, 2 August 1916. (Ces Mowthorpe Collection)

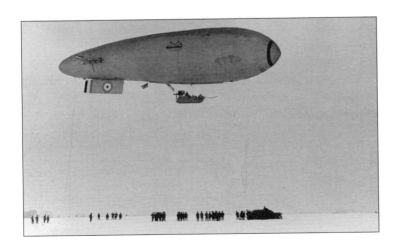

SSZ.3 while taking part in the trials of the single-wire mooring system, Pulham, 17 January 1918. The four guy-ropes — two for'd and two aft — are the handling guys. The mooring wire is just above the for'd guys. (JMB/GSL Collection)

SSZ.4 in flight, summer 1917. (Ces Mowthorpe Collection)

SSZ.5 taking off from Capel. Note the extra fin, complete with roundel. This was probably cannibalized from another 'Zero'. (W.J. Pullen via Brian Turpin)

SSZ.6 being assembled at Polegate, July 1917. Note the tail plane/elevators, not yet rigged but lying in the rear corner of the shed. (Ces Mowthorpe Collection)

1918. Hours flown: 311 hours 1917, 984 hours 1918. Deflated 25 December 1918. Deleted Luce Bay October 1919. No photograph of SSZ.12 can be traced.

SSZ.13
Assembled at Luce Bay. Trials 3 August 1917. Served at Luce Bay. Wrecked and deflated after engine trouble at Castle Head 30 August 1918, crew saved. Hours flown: 272 hours 1917, 859 hours 1918. Deleted Luce Bay 30 August 1918, 'wrecked at sea'.

SSZ.14
Assembled at Mullion. Trial flight 28 July 1917. Served at Mullion. Trial landing at Tresco, Scilly Isles, 25 August 1917. On 27 October 1917 drifted across Channel because engine failed (broken shaft), landed in trenches at Montreivil, France, 300 miles from base at Laira. Force landed in Toller Wood October 1918. Hours flown: 215 hours 1917, 615 hours 1918. Deflated 7 November 1918. Deleted Mullion October 1919.

SSZ.15
Assembled at Mullion. Trials 10 August 1917. Served at Mullion. To Toller(?) 13 April 1918. Lost at sea 2 miles south of Exmouth, captained by Lt G.R.J. Parkinson. Hours flown: 215 hours 1917, 195 hours 1918. Deleted Mullion 13 April 1918, lost at sea.

SSZ.16
Assembled at Pembroke. Trials 19 August 1917. Served at Pembroke. On 7 December 1917 sighted and attacked with machine-gun fire a German U-boat which had opened fire on the airship. Hours flown: 477 hours 1917, 930 hours 1918. Deflated 29 January 1919. Deleted Pembroke October 1919.

SSZ.17
Assembled at Pembroke. Trials 7 August 1917. Served at Pembroke. Destroyed by fire

in shed 3 January 1918. Hours flown: 448 hours 1917, 53 hours 1918. Deleted Pembroke 22 January 1918, destroyed by fire.

SSZ.18
Assembled at Folkestone. Trials 23 August 1917. Served at Folkestone. Hours flown: 135 hours 1917, 692 hours 1918. Deflated 13 December 1918. Deleted Folkestone October 1919. No photograph of SSZ.18 can be traced.

SSZ.19
Assembled at Polegate. Trials 6 October 1917. Served at Polegate. Hours flown: 146 hours 1917, 853 hours 1918. Deflated 28 January 1919. Deleted Polegate October 1919.

SSZ.20
Assembled at Luce Bay. Trials 19 October 1917. Served at Luce Bay. Hours flown: 154 hours 1917, 1,263 hours 1918. Deflated 5 February 1919. Deleted Luce Bay October 1919.

SSZ.21 AND SSZ.22
Both built at Wormwood Scrubs. Both sold to French Government. Left by air. It is believed that this served as their trials flight. Dimensions as all 'SSZ' ships. No photographs of SSZ.21 and SSZ.22 have been traced.

SSZ.23
Built at Wormwood Scrubs. Trials 2 January 1918. To Cranwell from Wormwood Scrubs December 1917. To Howden from Cranwell 9 March 1918. A 25 hour flight was made by Ensign Barnes USN on 29/30 May 1918. It was an old envelope of SSZ.23 which was being attached to a 'spare' car which caught fire and caused the conflagration which destroyed R.27 at RNAS Howden on 16

SSZ.7 taking off from Polegate, 10 July 1917.
(The Royal Aeronautical Society)

SSZ.9 after an accident at Polegate, 13 November
1917. (The Royal Aeronautical Society)

The car of SSZ.13. (Fleet Air Arm Museum; neg.
no. A/SHIP/134)

SSZ.14 being walked out, possibly at Mullion. (Fleet Air Arm Museum; neg. no. A/SHIP/351)

SSZ.15 at Mullion. (Fleet Air Arm Museum; neg. no. A/SHIP/363)

SSZ.16 flying over St David's. (Fleet Air Arm Museum; neg. no. A/SHIP/323)

SSZ.17 being hauled down at Pembroke, 1917. The handling-guys are in the hands of the handling crew, and the engineer is switching everything off. (Fleet Air Arm Museum; neg. no. A/SHIP/350)

August 1918. Car dispatched to America 4 August 1918, from Howden. Hours flown 1918: 336 hours.

SSZ.24

Built at Wormwood Scrubs. To US Government. Packed and shipped direct to USA November 1917. Its subsequent history is unknown. Dimensions and engine as all 'SSZs'. No photograph of SSZ.24 can be traced.

SSZ.25

Built at Wormwood Scrubs. Trials 15 December 1917. To Mullion from Wormwood Scrubs 15 December 1917. Broke loose from moorings in gale and wrecked 20 January 1918. Hours flown: 15 hours 1917, 42 hours 1918. Deleted Mullion 4 February 1918, replaced.

SSZ.26

Built at Wormwood Scrubs. Trials 22 January 1918. To Folkestone from Wormwood Scrubs 29 January 1918. Abandoned at sea on 27 February 1918, pilot and crew picked up by destroyer. Hours flown 1918: 90 hours. Deleted Folkestone 27 February 1918, lost at sea.

SSZ.27

Built at Wormwood Scrubs (time to build stated as 7–8 days). To Polegate from Wormwood Scrubs 15 February 1918. To Mullion from Polegate 25 March 1918. In collision with a trawler on 12 April 1918. According to B.G. Turpin's records, SSZ.27 sighted a mine near a trawler. The trawler fired at the mine but ricochets punctured SSZ.27's envelope, causing a loss of gas and collapse into the sea! The trawler salvaged the airship. Back in service in May 1918. Hours flown 1918: 782 hours. Deflated 10 December 1918. Deleted October 1919.

SSZ.28

Built at Wormwood Scrubs. Trials 17 February 1918. To Polegate from Wormwood Scrubs 17 February 1918. Made a flight of 26 hours 10 minutes on 26/27 June 1918 (Lt Protheroe). Hours flown 1918: 931 hours. Deflated 29 January 1919. Deleted Polegate October 1919.

SSZ.29

Built at Wormwood Scrubs. Trials 27 February 1918. To Folkestone from Wormwood Scrubs. Hours flown 1918: 871 hours. Deflated 24 January 1919. Deleted Folkestone October 1919.

SSZ.30

Built at Wormwood Scrubs. Trials 27 February 1918. To Polegate from Wormwood Scrubs 27 February 1918 (captained by Lt Meady). Hours flown 1918: 794 hours. Deflated 20 January 1919. Deleted Polegate October 1919.

SSZ.31

Built at Wormwood Scrubs. Trials 14 March 1918. To Howden from Wormwood Scrubs 10 April 1918. To Anglesey from Howden 1 August 1918. Hours flown: 313 hours 1918, 9 hours 1919. Deflated 24 January 1919. No photograph of SSZ.31 can be traced.

SSZ.32

Built at Wormwood Scrubs. Trials 14 March 1918. To Howden from Wormwood Scrubs 14 March 1918 (Capt G. Meager). Envelope torn by collision with trees on hillock at Lowthorpe (Capt Meager) on 19 May 1918. Wrecked at Kirkleatham 6 October 1918 on last flight; returned to Howden by rail. Hours flown 1918: 246 hours. Deleted Howden October 1919.

SSZ.33

Built at Wormwood Scrubs. Trials 21 March 1918. To Howden from Wormwood Scrubs

SSZ.19 landing at Polegate, 1917. (Fleet Air Arm Museum; neg. no. A/SHIP/371)

SSZ.20 preparing for patrol, Luce Bay, 1918. The captain was Flt Sub Lt Crump. (Flt Sub Lt Crump)

SSZ.23 in flight. (Ces Mowthorpe Collection)

SSZ.25, Mullion, 1917. Note the two 110 lb bombs on racks. There is also a camera mounted on the side. Little use was made of this latter fitting, so on later 'Zeros' the equipment was not fitted. (Ces Mowthorpe Collection)

SSZ.26 preparing for her trial flight, Wormwood Scrubs, 22 January 1918. (The Royal Aeronautical Society)

SSZ.27 in her shed at Mullion. Note the 110 lb bomb slung from the aft bomb rack. (Ces Mowthorpe Collection)

SSZ.28 at a mooring-out site. (The Royal Aeronautical Society)

SSZ.29 at Capel, 22 October 1916. (Fleet Air Arm Museum; neg. no. A/SHIP/359)

via Pulham 21 March 1918. To Anglesey from Howden 1 August 1918. Hours flown: 552 hours 1918, 1 hour 15 minutes 1919. Deflated Anglesey January 1919.

SSZ.34
Built at Wormwood Scrubs. Trials 21 March 1918. To Anglesey from Wormwood Scrubs via Cranwell 21 March 1918 and Howden 23 March 1918. Hours flown 1918: 859 hours 30 minutes. Deflated 26 November 1918.

SSZ.35
Built at Wormwood Scrubs. Trials 23 March 1918. To Anglesey from Wormwood Scrubs via Pulham 23 March 1918 and Howden 24 March 1918. On 26 April 1918 suffered engine failure over sea, towed by trawler to Llandudno beach, repaired in situ and flown out (Capt Williams). Made flight of 26 hours 10 minutes on 28/29 June 1918 (Capt Williams) at Anglesey. Lost at sea owing to torn envelope (cause unknown) 17 October 1918. Sunk 15 miles northwest of Holyhead, crew saved. Hours flown: 822 hours. Deleted October 1918.

SSZ.36
Built at Wormwood Scrubs. Trial flight 2 April 1918. To Folkestone from Wormwood Scrubs 2 April 1918. Moored out at Godmersham Park on 22 June 1918. In October 1918 a defective envelope caused crash into trees on landing at Capel. Deflated 1 November 1918. Hours flown: 644 hours. Deleted October 1919.

SSZ.37
Built at Wormwood Scrubs. Trials 2 April 1918. To Pembroke from Wormwood Scrubs 2 April 1918. Force landed near Mumbles 11 August 1918. Deflated but crew uninjured. Towing trials with PL.61 on 18 November 1918. Hours flown: 675 hours 30 minutes. Deflated 29 January 1919. Deleted October 1919.

SSZ.38
Built at Wormwood Scrubs. Trials 9 April 1918. To Howden from Wormwood Scrubs via Cranwell 20 May 1918 (Flt Lt Sparrow). Envelope torn by trees at Lowthorpe 28 June 1918, self-deflated owing to defective envelope. Hours flown: 48 hours. Deleted Howden 16 August 1918, destroyed by fire.

SSZ.39
Built at Wormwood Scrubs. Trials 12 April 1918. To Polegate from Wormwood Scrubs, after accident to controls, on 7 June 1918. On 11–13 August 1918 made flight of 50 hours 55 minutes (1,000 miles) captained by Lt Bryan. Last flight in November 1918. Hours flown: 856 hours. Deflated 29 January 1919.

SSZ.40
Built at Wormwood Scrubs. Trials 12 April 1918. To Mullion from Wormwood Scrubs via Polegate 13 April 1918. Force landed at Leedstown. Hours flown: 463 hours. Deleted October 1919.

SSZ.41
Built at Wormwood Scrubs. Trials 20 April 1918. To Polegate from Wormwood Scrubs. Hours flown 1918: 760 hours. Deflated 28 January 1919. No photograph of SSZ.41 can be traced.

SSZ.42
Built at Wormwood Scrubs. Approximate time to build was 62 days. Trials 25 April 1918. To Polegate from Wormwood Scrubs 25 April 1918. To Mullion from Polegate 26 April 1918. Force landed Ilford Camo near Christchurch, so arrived Mullion 6 May 1918 by rail. New envelope received 17 June 1918. Hours flown: 580 hours. Deflated 7 November 1918 owing to defective envelope. Deleted October 1919.

SSZ.30 moored-out in woods near Polegate, 1918. Note that the car is out of sight in a 'pit'; this was dug to bring the envelope closer to ground level for repairs and protection. (JMB/GSL Collection)

SSZ.32 (top) in RNAS mooring-out station, May 1918. SSZ.38 is alongside. Although the station was made to house only two 'Zeros', three could be accommodated. (Ces Mowthorpe Collection)

SSZ.33 preparing for flight at RNAS Malahide, 1918. (Fleet Air Arm Museum; neg. no. A/SHIP/166)

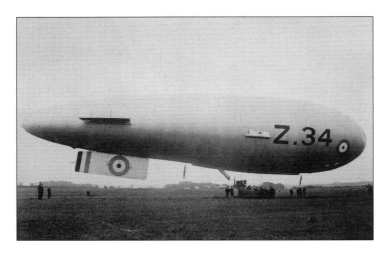

SSZ.34 preparing for take-off from, possibly, Cranwell, March 1918. (Fleet Air Arm Museum; neg. no. A/SHIP/348)

SSZ.35 preparing to take off from Anglesey, April 1918. The pilot was T.B. Williams. (Ces Mowthorpe Collection)

SSZ.36 caught in trees at Goodmersham Park, near Capel (Folkestone). (W.J. Pullen via Brian Turpin)

SSZ.37 exercising with patrol boat PC-1 in the Channel. (Ces Mowthorpe Collection)

SSZ.42 landing at Laira mooring-out site, near Mullion, 1918. (Fleet Air Arm Museum; neg. no. A/SHIP/370)

SSZ.43 in a mooring-out site near Polegate. (Fleet Air Arm Museum; neg. no. A/SHIP/349A)

SSZ.39 being prepared for flight. (Fleet Air Arm Museum; neg. no. A/SHIP/372)

SSZ.40 climbing away, possibly from Mullion. (Fleet Air Arm Museum; neg. no. A/SHIP/347)

SSZ.43
Built at Wormwood Scrubs. Trials 2 May 1918. To Polegate from Wormwood Scrubs 2 May 1918. Hours flown: 566 hours. Deflated 12 December 1918. Deleted October 1919.

SSZ.44
Built at Wormwood Scrubs. Trials 8 May 1918. To Polegate from Wormwood Scrubs 8 May 1918. Last flight November 1918. Hours flown 1918: 373 hours. Deflated 18 January 1919. Deleted October 1919. No photograph can be traced of SSZ.44.

SSZ.45
Built at Wormwood Scrubs. Trials 10 May 1918. To Mullion from Wormwood Scrubs, via Polegate, 10 May 1918. Force landed at Toller, near Bridport, July 1918. The observer (J. Owner) was hurled through the front of the car and sustained slight injuries. The pilot (Lt Savage) and engineer (H. Jobson) had more serious injuries. J. Owner staggered to the nearest post office where he had great difficulty in persuading the post mistress to allow him to make a free emergency call! Last flight November 1918. Hours flown: 503 hours. Deflated 3 December 1918. Deleted October 1919.

SSZ.46
Built at Wormwood Scrubs. Trials 15 May 1918. To Folkestone from Wormwood Scrubs 15 May 1918. Last flight November 1918. Hours flown 1918: 648 hours. Deflated 29 January 1919. Deleted October 1919.

SSZ.47
Built at Wormwood Scrubs. Trials 16 May 1918. To Mullion from Wormwood Scrubs via Polegate 17 May 1918. Last flight November 1918. Hours flown 1918: 380 hours. Deflated 5 January 1919. Deleted October 1919.

SSZ.48
Built at Wormwood Scrubs. Trials 16 May 1918. To Polegate from Wormwood Scrubs 17 May 1918. Force landed Tangmere airfield, engine unserviceable. Deflated. Force landed Horton Common, 'ripped', 20 September 1918. Hours flown 1918: 554 hours. Deflated 26 January 1919. Deleted October 1919.

SSZ.49
Built at Wormwood Scrubs. Trials 27 May 1918. To Mullion from Wormwood Scrubs via Polegate. Lost at sea 2 September 1918. Hours flown: 350 hours. Deleted 2 September 1918, lost at sea.

SSZ.50
Built at Kingsnorth. Trials 13 March 1918. To Anglesey from Kingsnorth 13 March 1918. Balloon-landing at night, when 'ripped', on 1 April 1918 at Malahide. Damaged by gale 4 October 1918. Force landed Aberayon 18 November 1918. Hours flown: 773 hours 1918, 1 hour 30 minutes 1919. Deflated 24 January 1919.

SSZ.51
Built at Kingsnorth. Trials 13 March 1918. Anglesey from Kingsnorth 13 March 1918. Envelope torn by propeller, ripped 2 April 1918. Force landed Iselo and ripped 5 April 1918. Crew saved by USS *Downs* when lost at sea 15 September 1918. Hours flown: 655 hours. Deleted Anglesey 15 September 1918, lost at sea.

SSZ.52
Built at Kingsnorth. Trials 17 March 1918. To Pembroke from Kingsnorth 17 March 1918. Last flight November 1918. Hours flown: 702 hours. Deflated 23 January 1919. Deleted October 1919.

SSZ.45 after her forced landing at Toller Down, near Bridport, Dorset. (JMB/GSL Collection)

SSZ.46 in flight. (Airship Heritage Trust (Focas))

SSZ.49 in flight near Polegate. (JMB/GSL Collection)

SSZ.47 being deflated at a mooring-out site near Mullion. (Fleet Air Arm Museum; neg. no. A/SHIP/346)

The car of SSZ.48. Note the Army corporal — an extra hand on this three-seater airship! (Fleet Air Arm Museum; neg. no. A/SHIP/327)

SSZ.50 climbing away. (Fleet Air Arm Museum;
neg. no. A/SHIP/345)

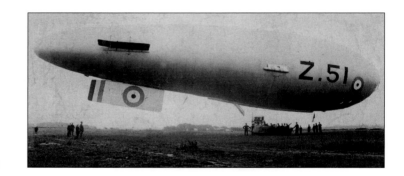

SSZ.51 preparing for flight, Anglesey, 1918.
(Fleet Air Arm Museum; neg. no. A/SHIP/358)

SSZ.52 in flight. (Fleet Air Arm Museum; neg. no.
A/SHIP/356)

SSZ.53

Built at Kingsnorth. Trials 21 March 1918. To Pembroke from Kingsnorth 21 March 1918. Last flight December 1918. Hours flown: 917 hours. Deflated 15 January 1919. Deleted October 1919.

SSZ.54

Built at Kingsnorth. Trials 8 April 1918. To Howden from Kingsnorth 8 April 1918. Envelope damaged by trees at Lowthorpe 3 June 1918 (Capt G. Meager). Hours flown: 201 hours. Destroyed by fire at Howden 16 August 1918. Deleted 16 August 1918.

SSZ.55

Built at Kingsnorth. Trials 8 April 1918. To Howden from Kingsnorth 3 June 1918. Force landed Skelfley Park 6 June 1918 (Capt Meager). Damaged in storm at Kirkleatham 22 June 1918. New car fitted at Howden overnight 22/23 June 1918. Deflated 13 October 1918. Deleted October 1919. Hours flown: 153 hours. B.G. Turpin records that SSZ.55 was initially retained at Kingsnorth for tests with 'experimental planes', flying 5 hours with them in May 1918.

SSZ.56

Built at Kingsnorth. Trials 18 April 1918. To Pembroke from Kingsnorth 18 April 1918. Last flight November 1918 at Howden. Hours flown: 539 hours. Deflated 25 November 1918. Deleted October 1919. No photograph of SSZ.56 can be traced.

SSZ.57

Built at Kingsnorth. Trials 25 April 1918. To Longside from Kingsnorth via Cranwell and Howden 25 April 1918. 'Ripped' after breaking away at Auldbar 2 November 1918. Deflated 8 November 1918. Deleted October 1919. Hours flown: 261 hours.

SSZ.58

Built at Kingsnorth. Trials 25 April 1918. To Longside from Kingsnorth via Howden 25 April 1918. Made forced landing in fog 9 miles from station 9 July 1918. Hours flown 1918: 397 hours. Deflated 21 January 1919. Deleted October 1919.

SSZ.59

Built at Kingsnorth. Trials 27 April 1918. To East Fortune from Kingsnorth via Cranwell and Howden 27 April 1918. To Chathill 2 November 1918. Deflated in gale. Force landed East Fortune 30 December 1918. Hours flown 1918: 174 hours. Deflated 31 December 1918. Deleted October 1919.

SSZ.60

Built at Kingsnorth. Trials 27 April 1918. To Cranwell from Kingsnorth 27 April 1918. East Fortune from Cranwell 20 May 1918. Hours flown: 194 hours 1918, 1 hour 30 minutes 1919.

SSZ.61

Built at Kingsnorth. Trials 4 May 1918. To Cranwell from Kingsnorth 4 May 1918. Last flight August 1918. Hours flown: 320 hours. Deflated 2 January 1919. No photograph of SSZ.61 can be traced.

SSZ.62

Built at Kingsnorth. Trials 9 May 1918. To Howden from Kingsnorth via Pulham and Cranwell 9 May 1918. Damaged in gale at Kirkleatham and deflated 17 June 1918. Slightly damaged by fire 16 August 1918. Last flight June 1918. Hours flown 1918: 69 hours.

SSZ.63

Built at Kingsnorth. Trials 10 May 1918. To Howden from Kingsnorth via Cranwell 10 May 1918. To Lowthorpe from Howden (Capt G. Meager) 23 May 1918. Envelope

Inflating the envelope of the SSZ.53 in the shed at Pembroke, 1918. (Fleet Air Arm Museum; neg. no. A/SHIP/357)

SSZ.54 in the 'Coastal' shed at Howden, 1918.
(Airship Heritage Trust (Focas))

SSZ.55 being hauled down by a landing party after
a flight, Howden, 30 May 1918. (The Royal
Aeronautical Society)

SSZ.57 being walked out of the shed. (JMB/GSL
Collection)

SSZ.58 over the North Sea near Longside. Note the 'weathered' condition of the envelope, ready for replacement. Active non-rigids went through about two envelopes a year by 1918. (JMB/GSL Collection)

SSZ.59 landing on aircraft carrier HMS *Furious*, summer 1918. Note the pristine condition of the envelope compared with that of the SSZ.58. (Ces Mowthorpe Collection)

SSZ.59 landing aboard HMS *Furious*. SSZ.60 is circling above. (Fleet Air Arm Museum; neg. no. A/SHIP/114)

and planes destroyed by fire 16 August 1918. Last flight June 1918. Hours flown: 110 hours. Deleted October 1919. No photograph of SSZ.63 can be traced.

SSZ.64

Built at Kingsnorth. Trials 11 May 1918. To Howden from Kingsnorth 11 May 1918. Last flight November 1918. Hours flown: 325 hours. Deflated 24 January 1919. Deleted 1919.

SSZ.65

Built at Kingsnorth. Trials 20 May 1918. To Longside from Kingsnorth via Pulham, Cranwell and Howden 20 May 1918. Flew 535 miles in 17 hours 44 minutes on 13 November 1918 with Lt Anderson as captain. Hours flown: 252 hours 1918, 2 hours 1919. Deflated 21 January 1919. Deleted October 1919.

SSZ.66

Built at Kingsnorth. Trials 22 May 1918. To Longside from Kingsnorth via Howden and East Fortune 22 May 1918. Force landed at McDuff 6 July 1918. Force landed at Arbratha 26 August 1918. Last flight December 1918. Hours flown 1918: 159 hours. Deflated 20 January 1919. Deleted October 1919. No photograph of SSZ.66 can be traced.

SSZ.67

Built at Kingsnorth. Trials 22 May 1918. To Pembroke from Kingsnorth 22 May 1918. On 28 July 1918 landed heavily and envelope torn by propeller. Last flight December 1918. Hours flown 1918: 639 hours. Deflated 27 January 1919. Deleted October 1919.

SSZ.68

Built at Wormwood Scrubs. No trials. Shipped to Kassandra, with SSZ.70, on SS *Teenkai* 24 August 1918. B.G. Turpin records

SSZ.68 made a one hour trial flight at Wormwood Scrubs on 30 May 1918, prior to deflation and packaging. Returned due to Armistice, still in packages, and was reduced to salvage. No photograph of SSZ.68 can be traced.

SSZ.69

Built at Wormwood Scrubs. Trials 26 June 1918. To Folkestone from Wormwood Scrubs 26 June 1918. Hours flown: 495 hours 1918, 30 minutes 1919. Deflated 19 January 1919. Deleted October 1919. No photograph of SSZ.69 can be traced.

SSZ.70

Built at Wormwood Scrubs. No trials? Shipped to Kassandra on SS *Teenkai* 24 August 1918.

SSZ.71

Built at Kingsnorth. Trials 7 December 1918. To Pulham from Kingsnorth 7 December 1918. Hours flown: 5 hours 1918, 4 hours 1919. Deflated 18 March 1919. Deleted October 1919.

SSZ.72

Built at Kingsnorth. Trials 12 November 1918. To Anglesey from Kingsnorth via Cranwell and Howden 12 November 1918. Hours flown 1918: 55 hours, in November only. Deflated 26 November 1918. No photograph of SSZ.72 can be traced.

SSZ.73

Assembled at Anglesey. Car arrived Anglesey 27 August 1918. First flight 7 September 1918. Flown under Menai bridge by Maj Elmhirst (CO Anglesey) after Armistice day, November 1918. Hours flown 1918: 232 hours. Deflated 24 January 1919. The feat of flying beneath the Menai bridge is worth telling, from *Recollections* by Air Marshal Sir Thomas Elmhirst KBE, CB, AFC. At an

SSZ.62 taking off from Kingsnorth for Howden, via Pulham and Cranwell, 9 May 1918. (The Royal Aeronautical Society)

SSZ.64 being walked out onto the field at Howden, 1918. Note the nose of R.26 in the shed on the left. (Fleet Air Arm Museum; neg. no. A/SHIP/80)

SS.65 landing at Longside. (Ces Mowthorpe Collection)

SSZ.67 in flight. (Fleet Air Arm Museum; neg. no. A/SHIP/355)

SSZ.70 at the Crystal Palace Exhibition, 1919. This airship never flew. With the SSZ.68 she was packaged (see text, p. 105) but was returned in the original packaging because of the Armistice. Her car was later displayed at Crystal Palace. (Ces Mowthorpe Collection)

SSZ.71 being prepared for flight at Pulham, January 1919. (Ces Mowthorpe Collection)

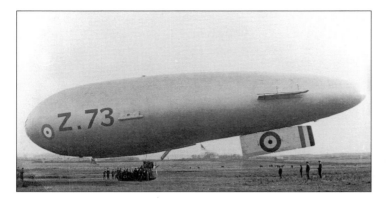

SSZ.73, based at Anglesey and Malahide. Her captain was Capt Elmhirst. (Ces Mowthorpe Collection)

Bochyn Wood mooring-out station near Mullion, November 1918. The airship in the foreground is thought to be SSZ.75. (Note the pit dug for the car.) The SST moored in the background is believed to be SST-2, which was at Mullion at this time. (Ces Mowthorpe Collection)

SSZ.77 in flight over Kingsnorth, January 1917. (Ces Mowthorpe Collection)

Armistice night party with his senior naval officer, Capt Gordon Campbell VC, Maj Elmhirst was asked by Campbell if such a flight was possible. After suggesting it was – subject to a proper reconnaissance – Capt Campbell replied: 'If you decide on it I will come with you as Observer'. Maj Elmhirst measured the height above low water and the bridge roadway, then reported that he would attempt it on the first occasion of suitable weather. Two or three mornings later, the weather and tide were in order and Capt Campbell arrived at dawn to find SSZ.73 on the Anglesey field, with its engine running. Approaching the bridge, Maj Elmhirst stopped the ship, head to wind (what little there was) and 'ballasted up'. Over the cockpit side he then lowered a small sandbag on a length of cord, measured to allow safe passage under the bridge. Then, in exact trim and equilibrium, he opened the throttle to give approximately 40 m.p.h. and steered for the centre of the bridge, with the sandbag bouncing on the water. Increasing to full speed so that he had full elevator control, Elmhirst guided SSZ.73 safely beneath. The reader should bear in mind that unlike an ordinary aeroplane, an airship pilot cannot see above, because of the envelope!

SSZ.74

Built at Kingsnorth. Trials 6 November 1918. To Folkestone from Kingsnorth 6 November 1918. Hours flown 1918: 30 hours. Deflated 23 January 1919. Deleted October 1919. No photograph of SSZ.74 can be traced.

SSZ.75

Built at Kingsnorth. Trials 9 November 1918. To Mullion from Kingsnorth 9 November 1918. Forced landing at Padstow 21 December 1918. Hours flown 1918: 43 hours. Deflated 22 December 1918. Deleted October 1919. B.G. Turpin records that the car of this 'Zero' was, like many others, built at Wormwood Scrubs. Although this was the final 'Zero' car built there, Kingsnorth completed two more 'Zeros'.

SSZ.76

Built at Kingsnorth. Trials 13 November 1918. To Pembroke from Kingsnorth 13 November 1918. Hours flown 1918: 13 hours. Deflated 15 January 1919. Deleted October 1919. B.G. Turpin records that Capt Sydney Taylor made the flight from Kingsnorth to Pembroke on 13 November 1918 in 6 hours 10 minutes. According to his logbook, this was Capt Taylor's last flight. No photograph of SSZ.76 can be traced.

SSZ.77

Built at Kingsnorth. Trials 23 January 1919. To Pulham from Kingsnorth 23 January 1919. Hours flown 1919: 5 hours. Deflated 21 February 1919. Deleted October 1919.

CHAPTER 7

THE 'SSES' AND 'SSTS'

THE 'SSE' CLASS

With the 'Zeros' well established in service, a slightly larger but equally useful non-rigid with twin-engined reliability and power was sought. The result was three airships prefixed 'SSE' (SS Experimental).

The early history of the 'SSE' class is shrouded in mystery. Some sources state that the SSE–1 was built at Cranwell. Admiralty records clearly state that it was Wormwood Scrubs, and name a 'Jones' as participating. She was damaged landing from her maiden flight to Pulham, classed as 'unsuitable' and deleted two months later, after only four-and-a-quarter hours.

No date for her trials can be found but it cannot have been long before her flight to Pulham on 2 May 1918. Interestingly, SSE–3 – also built at Wormwood Scrubs and credited to W.S. Jones in Admiralty records – made her trials flight on 14 March 1918, as much as two months earlier!

Meanwhile, SSE–2 was being designed at Mullion under the supervision of Flt Lt R.S. Montagu. She was successful from the start and was known as the 'Mullion Twin'. SSE–2 became the prototype of the 'SST' class ships which were being produced in quantity when the Armistice was signed. Of the 115 'SSTs' planned, only thirteen were actually built.

Basically, all three SSE airships had twin engines slung outboard of the car on gantries, port and starboard, just aft of amidships, with fuel tanks slung from the envelopes. SSE–2 might have been fitted with 75 hp Rolls-Royce Hawks. All three could carry a crew of four or five. The car of SSE–2 was angular and similar

to the 'SSP' car, whereas that of SSE–3 was streamlined and slightly shorter. However, both SSE–2 and SSE–3 had strengthened car bottoms for landing, with a small skid right aft to hold the 'tapered' car horizontal on the ground.

Originally, SSE–2 and SSE–3 were fitted with an 85,000 cu ft envelope, but both were later given one of 100,000 cu ft. These envelopes had ballonets which could be inflated from either engine via a central air-scoop.

SSE–3 flew for a year at Pulham before deflation. Then, for reasons unknown, she was re-inflated and used as a training craft for the American crew at Howden who were being trained to take over the ill-fated R.38.

THE 'SSE' SHIPS

SSE–1
Built at Wormwood Scrubs. Capacity: 85–90,000 cu ft. Two 90 hp Curtiss engines. To Pulham from Wormwood Scrubs, via Kingsnorth, 17 April 1918; damaged while landing at Pulham 2 May 1918. Hours flown 1918: 4 hours 15 minutes. Deleted Pulham 9 July 1918. Originally designated SST–1, this ship became SSE–1 around June 1918, with MT–1 becoming SSE–2.

SSE–2
Built at Mullion. Capacity: 85–90,000 cu ft. Two 75 hp Rolls-Royce Hawk engines. Trials flight 4 March 1918. Force landed in mud on River Plym 15 March 1918. Rebuilt at Wormwood Scrubs 17 July 1918. Deflated 17 April 1919. Deleted October 1919. Hours flown: 57 hours. Originally known as MT–1

SST–1 (actually SSE–1) under construction at Wormwood Scrubs. SST–1 was built in competition to SSE–2 from Mullion. SSE–2 became SST–1, and it is believed that the SST–1 shown here became SSE–3 after minor modifications. (The Royal Aeronautical Society)

MT–1 ('Mullion Twin'), otherwise known as SSE–2, the prototype SST. MT–1 collapsed in the Plym while trying to land during a storm. (Fleet Air Arm Museum; neg. no. A/SHIP/365)

SSE–2 – the original 'Mullion Twin' and virtual prototype of the SST-class. (JMB/GSL Collection)

SSE–3 landing at Kingsnorth, 1918. (Ces Mowthorpe Collection)

The car and engines of SSE–3; note the curved and streamlined body. (Ces Mowthorpe Collection)

(Mullion Twin–1); after rebuilding at Wormwood Scrubs (her car being used as the model for the 'SST' class) she was re-designated SSE–2 around June 1918.

SSE–3

Built at Wormwood Scrubs. Capacity: 85–90,000 cu ft. Twin-engined. Trial flight 14 March 1918. Deflated Pulham 12 June 1919. Re-inflated at Pulham. Flown by Capt T.B. Williams 19 February 1920. Arrived Howden from Pulham to instruct American crew of R.38 on 8 March 1920. Made flights with Americans on 19 and 31 March and 7 and 20 June 1920. At some stage she was fitted with a new 100,000 cu ft envelope. This was the last British Naval non-rigid to fly, on 28 October 1920, prior to deflation and deletion.

THE 'SST' CLASS

The background to the 'SST' ships is set out in the history of SSE–2, the 'Mullion Twin'. Little further can be added except that most of the 'SSTs' were fitted sooner or later with the 100,000 cu ft envelope. The envelope capacity quoted for all non-rigids is that given in the Admiralty records. However sometimes this included the capacity of the ballonets, sometimes not – thus a range 85–90,000 cu ft, for example, is given. The 'SSTs', plus SSE–2 and SSE–3, were fitted originally with envelopes of 85,000 cu ft (total), later with ones of 100,000 cu ft (total) as required. These two sizes were a standard for RNAS non-rigids by late 1918. The thirteen 'SST' ships were numbered SST–1 to SST–14, SST–13 being omitted for reasons of superstition.

THE 'SST' SHIPS

Length: 165 ft
Height: 49 ft
Diameter: 35 ft 6 in

Engines: Two 100 hp Sunbeam or two 75 hp Rolls-Royce engines
Top speed: 57 m.p.h.
Gross lift: 3.1 tons
Disposable lift: 1.0 ton

SST–1

Built at Wormwood Scrubs. Credited to Flt Lt Montagu. Length 135 ft? Capacity: 100,000 cu ft, 4 ballonets. Trials 17 June 1918. To Folkestone 26 June 1918. To Kingsnorth 24 August 1918. To Folkestone 14 October 1918. Hours flown: 155 hours 1918, 3 hours 30 minutes 1919. Deflated Capel 7 April 1919.

SST–2

Built at Wormwood Scrubs. Capacity 90,000 cu ft, 4 ballonets. Trials 8 July 1918. To Polegate 8 July 1918. To Kingsnorth 28 July 1918. To Mullion (Toller) 17 October 1918. Hours flown: 74 hours 1918, 17 hours 1919. Deflated 28 January 1919.

SST–3

Built at Wormwood Scrubs. Capacity 85,000 cu ft, 4 ballonets. Trials 20 July 1918. To Howden 29 July 1918, captained by Sub Lt B. Harris. Hours flown: 131 hours 1918, 60 hours 1919. Deflated 18 June 1919.

SST–4

Built at Wormwood Scrubs. Capacity 90,000 cu ft, 4 ballonets. Trials 31 July 1918. To Howden 1 August 1918. Hours flown 1918: 189 hours. Deflated 31 October 1918.

SST–5

Built at Wormwood Scrubs. Capacity 85,000 cu ft, 4 ballonets. Howden 16 August 1918. Destroyed in gale 5 November 1918. Hours flown 1918: 196 hours. Deleted Howden 5 November 1918.

SST–6

Built at Wormwood Scrubs. Envelope capacity 90,000 cu ft, 4 ballonets. Not

SST–1 flying over Boulogne harbour accompanied by two 'Zeros', 27 November 1918. (The Royal Aeronautical Society)

SST–1, the first of the production 'Mullion Twins', about to take off on trials at Wormwood Scrubs, 17 June 1918. (Ces Mowthorpe Collection)

SST–2 in flight, Polegate, July 1918. (JMB/GSL Collection)

SST–3 in flight. (JMB/GSL Collection)

SST–4 taking off from Howden, 2 October 1918. (The Royal Aeronautical Society)

SST–5 at Kingsnorth, possibly during trials. (Cdr J. Havers via Brian Turpin)

SST–8 over Capel, 23 October 1918. (The Royal Aeronautical Society)

SST–9 arriving at Howden, 17 October 1918. (The Royal Aeronautical Society)

SST–11 at Kingsnorth, believed to be during trials. (Cdr J. Havers via Brian Turpin)

SST–12 arriving at Howden, 28 October 1918. (The Royal Aeronautical Society)

SST–14. (Fleet Air Arm Museum; neg. no. A/SHIP/360)

accepted Kingsnorth 29 August 1918. Caught fire after obvious engine trouble. Car fell from 400 ft, killing all crew: Capts Righton, Barlett and King, Sgt Cameron and Airman Cowen. Deleted 29 August 1918. No photograph of SST–6 has been traced.

SST–7
Built at Wormwood Scrubs. Length 135 ft. Capacity 90,000 cu ft, 4 ballonets. To Howden 29 September 1918. Hours flown 1918: 100 hours. Deflated January 1919. No photograph of SST–7 has been traced.

SST–8
Built at Wormwood Scrubs. Capacity 90,000 cu ft, 4 ballonets. Length 135 ft. To Folkestone 14 October 1918. Hours flown 1918: 94 hours. Deflated January 1919.

SST–9
Built at Wormwood Scrubs. Capacity 90,000 cu ft, 4 ballonets. To Howden 17 October 1918. Hours flown: 66 hours 1918, 32 hours 1919. Deflated 1 May 1919. Packed and sold to USA.

SST–10
Built at Wormwood Scrubs. Capacity 90,000 cu ft, 4 ballonets. To Howden 18 October 1918. Hours flown: 68 hours 1918, 55 hours 1919. Mine-clearing. Deflated 9 June 1919. No photograph of SST–10 has been traced.

SST–11
Built at Wormwood Scrubs. Capacity 90,000 cu ft, 4 ballonets. To Howden 26 October 1918. Hours flown: 33 hours 1918, 5 hours 1919. Packed and sold to the USA in June 1919.

SST–12.
Built at Wormwood Scrubs. Capacity 90,000 cu ft, 4 ballonets. To Howden 26 October 1918. Hours flown: 35 hours 1918, 5 hours 1919. Packed and sold to the USA in June 1919.

SST–14
Built at Wormwood Scrubs. Capacity 90,000 cu ft, 4 ballonets. To Pulham 16 May 1919. On 30 May 1919 made a 52 hour 15 minute flight (Capt S.E. Taylor DSC). The official records for this airship are clearly unreliable. They state that just 3 hours were flown in 1919, and that, although SST–14 was deflated on 13 June 1919, new top planes were fitted on 30 February 1920.

CHAPTER 8

THE SR-1

In the Mediterranean theatre, Britain's allies, the Italians, had considerable success with their semi-rigid 'M' class airships. These were capable of operating well up to 15,000 ft with a bomb-load in excess of half-a-ton. This suggested that the class would be suitable for the extended patrols that the Royal Navy made. Although negotiations to purchase an Italian 'M' class semi-rigid were begun in 1917, it was July 1918 before a British crew could be dispatched to Ciampino, near Rome, where the airship was built, to fly her back to England.

SR-1's maiden flight took place on 28 August 1918. She then completed a number of test flights, on which members of the British crew flew for experience, under the Italian captain's orders. After some ten flights, the SR-1 was accepted by Maj Cochrane (later Air Chief Marshal Sir Ralph Cochrane) on behalf of the Controller of Aircraft Production RAF, and handed over to her new 'skipper', Capt George Meager, who was to fly her home for the Admiralty. By this time, the ship had received her British service designation of SR-1.

A semi-rigid, SR-1 fell between the non-rigid blimps in use with the RNAS for submarine searching and the huge Zeppelin-type rigid airships that operated with a surface fleet for over 48 hours of continuous flying. Unfortunately, because of the many delays between ordering and delivery, the SR-1 was to prove outdated and be too late to take an active part in the First World War. However, with her triangular keel firmly fastened to the envelope, enclosed car and variable-pitch propellers, she was an aircraft

the like of which the RAF has not seen since!

SR-1's full-length triangular keel, with the apex at the bottom, was formed of alloy tubes connected by ball-joints that absorbed flexing. Surrounding this was the envelope, which had ballonets each side above the keel; around these was a hydrogen envelope of 441,000 cu ft capacity. The latter two items were integral and affixed with laces to the keel.

To the lower edge of the keel was a long fixed lower fin. On the stern post was a pair of 'biplane' elevators, the outboard extremities of which consisted of a pair of vertical rudders. These movable tail surfaces were referred to as the 'plane-cage'. Projecting to the rear of the lower fin, they were still inboard from the end of the envelope. On top of the envelope was a long fixed fin similar to the lower fin.

Of streamline shape with blunt stern, the envelope was of almost circular form but was attached directly to the canvas-covered keel, thus presenting a pear-shaped section when viewed from the front. Suspended slightly forward of amidships was an ugly, deep, but quite large enclosed car. This was rigged to the keel by innumerable suspension cables.

In flight, the car was about 15 ft below the keel, but because it was deep in proportion to its length and also had one of the airship's engines mounted on its roof, this large gap was not too obvious. A ladder joined the car to the keel, enabling crew to climb, via an internal fabric tube, onto the observation platform above the nose of the envelope.

The SR-1 differed from the Italian 'M' ships in having three engines. All other 'M'

SR–1 landing at Pulham, from Kingsnorth, 1918. Note the two external sleeping berths suspended from the envelope forward of the car. These were supposed to have been removed at Kingsnorth. (Imperial War Museum)

ships were powered by two 220 hp Italia engines (based on the Zeppelin Maybachs and built under licence) which were fitted onto platforms projecting outboard of the car, one each side, and completely open to the elements. On the fore-end of each platform was mounted a huge square radiator, 5 ft by 5 ft, at right-angles to the car side.

These two Italias drove one pusher propeller each, by means of a shaft over 15 ft long which projected a few feet astern of the car. Like the engines, this shaft was external and braced to the platform at suitable intervals. The two propellers onto which the shafts terminated were perhaps the most interesting feature of the SR–1. Four-bladed and 10 ft in diameter with square-cut tips, their variable pitch had six settings, from coarse to fine.

Because of the long delivery flight to England, SR–1 was fitted with a third engine for extra reliability and increased power. This was an Italian SPA–6a of 200 hp, driving a two-bladed pusher propeller. With a radiator in front, it was mounted in the open upon the car roof, on a braced and strutted platform about 4 ft high, to give the propeller the necessary clearance. After the SR–1 arrived at Pulham, and prior to her last two flights, this SPA engine was removed. Then she flew on her two Italias like other 'M' class airships.

The car itself was divided into several compartments. Forward was the control cabin containing two coxswains, the captain and all the flying controls. Behind and above was the engineers' space which was partially open to the elements in order that the engineers could climb out onto the engine platforms for servicing – in flight if necessary. Below and to the rear was a sound-proofed radio room for the W/T operator.

This left the remaining space for other crew requirements. The normal operating crew was eight but the car was still large enough to accommodate four or five passengers if required.

Another unusual feature of this airship was the two boat-like enclosed sleeping-berths suspended from the keel, forward of the car. Fitted for the delivery flight, the crew were kept so busy that they never used them! Below the car was a full-length fabric-covered 'bumping-bag' which cushioned landings and took the airship's weight when it was on the ground.

Originally, like all 'M' ships, SR-1 was fitted with a semi-automatic cannon in the nose of the car. This and other unnecessary items were removed immediately prior to the delivery flight on the orders of Capt Meager, in order to save weight. Meager estimated that the cannon weighed well over a hundred pounds. However, SR-1 still carried one machine-gun and ammunition in its upper observation platform.

The flight from Italy to England was the first direct flight in either direction between the countries at that period. This alone was proof of the capabilities of the ship and its crew.

The flight from Italy commenced in the early hours of the 28 October 1918 and took three-and-a-half days to complete. Landings were made at Aubagne, Lyons and St Cyr (Paris) in order to refuel and top up with hydrogen. Finally SR-1 touched down at Kingsnorth at 14.35 hours on 31 October 1918.

This remarkable flight was not without its difficulties. The SPA engine gave problems after the first few hours. Leaking oil from several places, it soon covered the roof of the car with a black film. It would not start at Lyons, the engineers eventually getting it to work after the flight had begun on the two Italias.

By far the most serious moment occurred a few hours later when the SR-1 was over the small French town of Chauffailles. The crew heard a loud crack and at the same time the SPA engine's note increased harshly. Chief officer T.B. Williams and second engineer Plt Off H. Leach ran up the ladder leading to the roof of the car to find the exhaust pipe had burnt through and broken off. The SPA was now emitting a stream of red-hot sparks into the slipstream and onto the petrol tank on the roof of the car below – and directly above was nearly half-a-million cubic feet of hydrogen! Only prompt action by the two crewmen in throwing the broken parts overboard and brushing the sparks off the petrol tank prevented disaster. Temporary repairs to the SPA were carried out at St Cyr, but it blew out a plug during the crossing of the Channel and had to be shut down for the rest of the flight.

The route across France had to be adhered to strictly. It was feared that the SR-1 might be mistaken for a German airship, so the French authorities provided a pilot of the French Airship Service, Lt Picard, who joined the SR-1 at Aubagne. Unfortunately, unfavourable headwinds up the Rhone valley necessitated an emergency landing at the airfield of Bron, near Lyons. Here the crew, who had already been active for over 24 hours without a break, had to refuel and re-gas from cans and cylinders.

However, they anticipated some respite at St Cyr, because there the SR-1 was to be serviced inside one of the French airship sheds while most of the crew had a well-earned rest. Unfortunately, wrong measurements had been given to St Cyr, so when the SR-1 landed the crew found the proposed shed too small. Once again she was serviced in the open and again her crew were unable to rest. Here Lt Picard left the ship – gloomily forecasting trouble!

Eight hours after leaving St Cyr, the airship landed at Kingsnorth – depositing a semi-conscious crew, deafened by the roar of the three motors surrounding them and filthy with engine oil from the overhead SPA, which had by this time soaked through the control car's canvas and was swilling around on the floor.

All the crew received decorations for this outstanding flight, including the Italian officer, Lt di Rossi, who had accompanied the British crew as a representative of the Italian Air Service. That the awards were deserved can be judged by the final words of Capt Meager's report: 'Only by Providence was the ship got through'.

The next few days were occupied in overhauling SR–1 at Kingsnorth, before leaving for her own station, Pulham, on 6 November 1918. Still on board was Lt di Rossi plus Col Cunningham, one of Britain's senior airship officers.

As Pulham was the Airship Experimental Station, SR–1 was soon scheduled for sundry 'improvements'. Although removal of the plane cage and a redesign of the car were mentioned, the cessation of hostilities prevented these being carried out, though the external sleeping-berths were removed at about this time.

SR–1's red-letter day came on 20 November 1918. Together with rigid R.26, she was detailed to accompany a flotilla of destroyers meeting the German submarine fleet which was steaming across the North Sea to surrender at Harwich. SR–1's complement of twelve for this flight included four passengers. Her next and final flight before deflation was on 7 December when she flew some Naval officers over the North Sea on 'experimental work'. Returning that evening, she was laid up and deflated. Her additional SPA–6a engine, together with its mounting, was removed.

During the summer of 1919, SR–1 was re-inflated at Pulham and carried out two more flights. Now without her third engine she was an ordinary Italian 'M' type again, and it was on the first of these flights that she created an endurance record for her class of 25 hours 20 minutes. By this time, parachutes had been issued to the airship branch and SR–1 was fitted with one per crew member.

Altogether SR–1 carried out twenty-two flights for the British airship service, including her delivery flight. She is recorded as having flown 54 hours 30 minutes in British service in 1918, and 40 hours 50 minutes in 1919. Her fastest recorded speed was 45.9 m.p.h.

CHAPTER 9

THE WARTIME RIGIDS

The story of the British rigid airship is a mixture of failure, bad planning, stubbornness, some success, and tragedy. The one redeeming feature is the expertise and sheer professional ability of the British airshipman, whatever his status.

Because British designs were essentially copies of the Zeppelins – with the possible exception of R.101 – this country's rigid airships were always several years behind German developments. Additionally, the German Government gave substantial support to the Zeppelin company, which built 130 Zeppelins; another twenty-four were constructed by the firm of Shutte-Lanz. Compare this with the eighteen rigids built in Britain. Here, Vickers, the one firm that could have built successful ships, was held back constantly by the Admiralty which, for reasons of its own, wished to control the lighter-than-air scene. Not until after the Battle of Jutland in 1916 was there any great demand for large rigids.

This was too late. The British '23' and '23x' classes were already outdated when they were conceived. Even with postwar knowledge of the Zeppelin, R.38, the only true postwar rigid prior to R.100 and R.101, was a disaster. While the later R.100 was undoubtedly successful, the R.101 – brilliant in concept – followed in R.38's disastrous footsteps.

Set against this must be the achievements. There was Vickers' quantum leap in just five years from the experimental No. 9r of 1914 to the superb R.80; R.34's double crossing of the Atlantic in 1919; the development of the mooring mast; the release and recapture of a De Havilland Hummingbird aircraft by R.33 – to mention but a few. These successes are even greater when it is realised that they were undertaken by an under-funded and often misunderstood minority!

THE SHIPS

On 22 August 1918 an Admiralty conference discussed new designs for the period 1919–20. As work had already begun both in design and construction for R.35–R.39, the 'R.35' class, it must be assumed that the conference were studying R.40–R.45, the 'R.40' class.

This was a purely British design, whose specification was 'To work with the Fleet for 72 hours minimum and 300 miles from base. To operate in 40 m.p.h. winds and give continuous Fleet cover for 30 days, operating a relay system.'

Shortly afterwards, the end of hostilities brought the whole airship programme to a halt, although work continued on rigids under construction. Early in 1919, when R.31 and R.32 had been completed and dispatched from Cardington, the Admiralty took over Short Brothers' works there, which had the largest construction shed. Short Brothers had been given R.38 (of the 'R.35' class) as its next order, and preliminary work had started on this ship.

Under Constructor-Commander Campbell, Cardington was reorganised: the design and ordering of components for R.40 (first of the 'R.40' class) was got underway, with the intention of utilising the same components as the proposed R.38.

Gradually, peacetime financial constraints brought the whole rigid airship programme to a halt. Then, in October 1919, the Admiralty succeeded in selling a British rigid airship to the American Navy. Consequently Constructor-Commander Campbell was given a free hand to design an airship to the Anglo-American specification. Scrapping work on R.40, Campbell proceeded to build R.38 – but this bore no relation to the original 'R.35' class R.38, started by Messrs Short Brothers!

The latest Vickers design took to the air on 19 July 1920. Designed by Barnes Wallis, this superb airship – sometimes referred to as a small '33' class – was given the number R.80!

HMA NO. 1 'MAYFLY'
No. 1 'Mayfly'
Length: 512 ft
Diameter: 61 ft 10 in
Engines: Two 200 hp Wolseleys

No. 1 'Mayfly' was built in a special hangar in the Cavendish Dock, Barrow-in-Furness, under a design team headed by Vickers' chief engineer, Mr Charles Robertson, and backed by Naval commanders Sueter and Schwann and Capt Bacon. The airship's specification was to fly at 40 knots for 24 hours, carry radio equipment, be capable of mooring on both water and land, and have a ceiling of 1,500 ft.

Regrettably the Navy insisted No. 1 should carry heavy naval equipment such as anchors and mooring chain, etc. This, together with a natural tendency to build in too much strength, made her far too heavy. Nevertheless, when No. 1 was taken out for mooring trials on 22 May 1911, she remained successfully moored to a lattice mast for nearly four days without damage in winds up to 45 m.p.h. She then returned to her hangar for major adjustments: i.e. removing excess weight, including her triangular keel, which left her framework distorted and badly weakened.

No. 1's frame was made of forty transverse twelve-sided rings, each connected by twelve longitudinals. This gave a cross-section which an American scientist, Dr A.F. Zahm, erroneously claimed was 40 per cent more efficient than that of the Zeppelins. Beneath the frame was a triangular keel with an amidships cabin.

Unfortunately, duralumin was chosen as the metal for the framework. This was a little-known alloy in 1908, and Vickers had considerable difficulty in working it. Originally the internal bracing wires were duralumin, but repeated breakages during construction meant they had to be replaced with steel.

The gas-bags, manufactured by Short Brothers, were of rubberised fabric imported from Germany. The outer covering was of silk, waterproofed using an aluminium-based dope. Inside were seventeen gas-bags of varying sizes, each with two valves (of Parseval design) at the top, one automatic, the other manual. The total volume was 663,500 cu ft.

At the stern were fixed stabilising fins with separate quadruple box rudders and triple elevators attached below their trailing edge. Additional triplane elevators and rudders were positioned behind the rear gondola. These control surfaces were not hinged but used Short's Reversible Patent Aerocurve, which flexed.

No. 1 had two mahogany open cars, or gondolas, sewn with copper wire, which could float on water. They were each fitted with 180 hp Wolseley 8-cylinder engines. The forward engine drove two 11 ft 10 in propellers on outriggers (replaced later by a single 10 ft diameter direct-drive propeller), and the rear engine drove a single 15 ft propeller. Initially, a water recovery apparatus which could utilise moisture from the exhaust gases was fitted to each engine. As the apparatus weighed nearly half-a-ton, it was removed to save weight.

Although inspired by the Zeppelins, No. 1's design was in fact very little influenced by the German airships. Had she not been so heavy and actually got airborne, much credit would have gone to her designers. In Naval records she is often referred to as HMS *Hermione* or the 'Hermione Airship'. In Admiralty records No. 1 first appears as the *Hermione* airship, so named because the Naval contingent overseeing the construction at Barrow, under Cdr Murray Sueter, were attached to HMS *Hermione*.

On 24 September 191, while leaving the hangar stern first, she was caught by a gust of wind. Poor handling by the unskilled handling party did not help matters, and No. 1 struck the hangar side and broke her back. She was then broken up.

HMA NO. 9r

Designed by Vickers chief designer H.B. Pratt and his assistant, Barnes Wallis, No. 9r was influenced greatly by secret French plans of the Zeppelin Z.IV which had force landed at Luneville on 3 April 1913. Although the order was placed on 10 June 1913 she was not completed until November 1916 owing to both political and Naval alterations. At one point during the war, work was actually suspended and the whole project halted!

No. 9r was very strongly built to withstand mishandling by unskilled crews. Constructed entirely of triangular-section duralumin girders, her cross-section was a seventeen-sided polygon with longitudinals at each 'corner'. From the two lowest longitudinals extended a triangular keel, forming a strong corridor which added strength and was the repository for ballast, fuel, stores, etc. Midway along was an expanded trapezium section which formed the crew's quarters and a wireless shack. Between each mainframe was a gas-bag made from rubberised cotton lined with goldbeaters skin. An access tube led from the keel to the gun platform on top of the hull.

As on all rigids, a walkway went aft from the gun platform to the tail where the hull was re-entered at the tail-gunner's position. Suspended from the keel were two cars or gondolas which contained the engines and the controls. Access from the keel was by open ladders.

No. 9r's tail surfaces were unusual. These consisted of a vertical fin and rudder on top, assisted by auxiliary rudders slightly to the rear, and horizontal fins and elevators assisted by auxiliary elevators below. All these auxiliary surfaces were removed after the first two flights.

Length: 526 ft
Diameter: 53 ft
Height: 76 ft
Envelope capacity: 846,000 cu ft, seventeen gas-bags
Engines: Four 180 hp Wolseleys; two were later removed and replaced by a single Zeppelin 240 hp Maybach
Top speed: 43 m.p.h.
Gross lift: 25.6 tons
Disposable lift: 3.8 tons

Completed 16 November 1916 but damaged control car bottom on leaving shed. Re-housed for repairs. Maiden flight 27 November 1916. On 13 December 1916 started speed trials but these terminated when her auxiliary rudders broke adrift. These were never refitted. Unable to lift her contract weight, she was further modified. A single 240 hp Maybach motor (from the crashed Zeppelin L.33) was fitted in place of the two Wolseleys in the rear car and she was re-bagged with lighter gas-bags. To Howden (Rigid Trials Flight) from Barrow 4 April 1917. To East Fortune 6 August 1917. To Howden 13 August 1917. On 29 September 1917 No. 9r carried out turning trials at Cranwell. At 17 knots with 20 degrees of helm her turning circle to starboard had a

No. 1r 'Mayfly' being towed out to a buoy and mast at Cavendish Dock, Barrow, for mooring-out trials, 22 May 1911. (Ces Mowthorpe Collection)

No. 1r 'Mayfly' with her back broken after being taken out of her floating shed at Cavendish Dock, Barrow, 24 September 1911. (Ces Mowthorpe Collection)

radius of 1,760 yd; to port under same conditions it was only 1,050 yd. The time taken to turn varied between 11 minutes and 20 minutes. On 15 October 1917 she flew to Cranwell. Diverted to Howden on 29 October 1917 due to bad weather; damaged while entering shed. At Pulham 20 February 1918. Carried out mooring experiments in the Wash (to a buoy) and on Pulham airfield using the 'three-wire' system. After four days the girders in the nose sheered and she was taken inside. Hours flown: 155 hours 6 minutes 1917, 33 hours 10 minutes 1918. Her seventeenth patrol, on 21/22 July 1917, lasted 26 hours 45 minutes, a British record. Deleted 28 June 1918. The CO at Pulham had 20 ft of her bow cut off and used it as a proboscian bandstand and rose-trellis!

HMA NO. 23r

The structure of the '23' class was basically the same as No. 9r, upon which they were based. An extra bay was inserted amidships and the nose and tail were widened. This allowed the insertion of an extra gas-bag which increased the capacity and lift. The keel had a widened section amidships, 45 ft long, incorporating a bomb room, officers' and men's quarters, a wireless shack and a lavatory aft. The normal complement was sixteen, although two more could be accommodated.

From this keel were suspended three cars. The forward car contained the control room and one engine. The amidships car contained two engines, each driving its own propeller, while the after car was similar to the fore car, being fitted with emergency controls and one engine. The fore and aft engines each drove two propellers, all of which were capable of swivelling through 180 degrees. Fuel was in twenty 60 gal capacity tanks situated along the keel. There were also twelve water ballast bags each of 28 gal capacity. The tail surfaces

were the (by now) usual cruciform elevators and rudders.

Builder: Messrs Vickers
Length: 535 ft
Height: 75 ft
Diameter: 53 ft
Capacity: 942,000 cu ft, eighteen gas-bags
Engines: Four 250 hp Rolls-Royce engines
Top speed: 52 m.p.h.
Gross lift: 28.5 tons
Disposable lift: 6.5 tons

Trial flight at Barrow 19 September 1917. With gross lift under 6 tons, the dynamos, bomb gear and furniture were removed. A 240 hp Maybach from the crashed Zeppelin L.33 was fitted in place of the Rolls-Royce, in a smaller rear car from which the emergency controls had been omitted. Arrived Howden from Barrow 15 October 1917. Arrived Pulham 29 October 1917. Overflew Buckingham Palace and Whitehall on mid-day 6 December 1917. Made an experimental flight of 40 hours 8 minutes on 30/31 May 1918, captained by Maj Little. Carried out experiments at Pulham with defensive armaments, including being fitted with a 2-pounder quick-firing gun on the upper platform. This gun was fired on several occasions as No. 23r cruised around the airfield. Three machine-guns were also carried. In July 1918 was fitted with 'Little-Crook Anchoring-Gear' for releasing aeroplanes in flight. A Sopwith Camel (carrying a dummy pilot) was released over Fens on 3 November 1918. Lt R.E. Keys DFC was the first pilot to accomplish this feat, landing successfully at Pulham. On 6 November 1918 two 'Ships Camels' were released, piloted by two officers from 212 Sqd RAF; No. 23r was captained by Flt Lt G.M. Thomas DFC. Overflew surrender of German U-boat fleet at Harwich November 1918. Her bows were strengthened and

No. 9r flying over the Vickers Works at Barrow, April 1917. Note the single propeller in the rear car denoting that the two original Wolseley engine have been replaced with the single German 240 hp Maybach, complete with its single 17 ft propeller (see text, p. 125). (Ces Mowthorpe Collection)

The rear car of No. 9r after two of its Wolseley engines were replaced by a single Maybach engine (see text, p. 125). (Ces Mowthorpe Collection)

HMA No. 23r, at Pulham, 1917. Note the caterpillar tractor — the same one is shown in the photograph of P.6. No. 23r must have been visiting Cranwell because she was 'on strength' at Pulham during this period. (JMB/GSL Collection)

wheels were fitted beneath the forward car for experiments with the three-wire mooring system at Pulham in March/April 1919. During this period No. 23 was fitted with special 'springs' to test sea-drogues in the Wash. Deleted September 1919. Hours flown: approximately 320 hours.

HMA NO. 24r
Builder: Messrs Beardmore
Length: 535 ft
Height: 75 ft
Diameter: 53 ft
Capacity: 942,000 cu ft, eighteen gas-bags
Engines: Four 250 hp Rolls-Royce engines
Top speed: 38 m.p.h.
Gross lift: 8.5 tons
Disposable lift: 6.0 tons
Structural details: as No. 23r

First flight 28 October 1917. Arrived East Fortune from Inchinnan 28 October 1917. Because No. 24r was so much heavier than her sisterships (attributed to Beardmore's using extra-strong rivets and fastenings, etc.), and because of the urgent need for her shed at Inchinnan for building R.34, the unusual step was taken of removing all machinery from the rear car – engine, propeller, etc. – to enable No. 24r to obtain the required lift to surmount the hills between Inchinnan and East Fortune. This reduced her top speed to approximately 30 m.p.h. The machinery was then replaced and No. 24r carried out her acceptance trials on 11 December 1917 at East Fortune. On one occasion she was caught in a mild gale near Bass Rock, where, for several hours, she could make no headway whatsoever – at times actually moving astern – due to complete failure of her port amidships engine. Arrived Howden 22 May 1918. Arrived Pulham 31 May 1918. Last flight made at Pulham June 1918. In March/April 1919 her bows were strengthened and nose-cone modified, extra ballast tanks were fitted and the centre car

removed for mooring-mast experiments at Pulham. Moored to Pulham 'high' mast (120 ft) 11–30 July 1919, 1 September–15 October 1919, 4 and 7 November. On 12 December 1919, after 63 days moored out in all weathers, No. 24r was returned to her shed in a 'bad condition' and later reduced to scrap. Deleted 31 December 1919 at Pulham. Hours flown: 10 hours 3 minutes 1917, 154 hours 7 minutes 1918, 28 minutes 1919.

HMA NO. 25r
Builder: Messrs Armstrong-Whitworth
Length: 535 ft
Height: 75 ft
Diameter: 53 ft
Total capacity 943,000 cu ft, eighteen gas-bags
Engines: Four 250 hp Rolls-Royce engines
Top speed: 52 m.p.h.
Gross lift: 28.5 tons
Disposable lift: 6.5 tons
Structural details: as No. 23r

Acceptance trials Howden 23 December 1917. Arrived Howden from Barlow 14 October 1917. Arrived Cranwell 5 April 1918 (Capt G.H. Scott, Chief Engineer Shotter). Arrived Pulham 5 July 1918. Hours flown: 6 hours 20 minutes 1917, 214 hours 45 minutes 1918, none 1919(?). Carried out experimental tests at Cranwell May–July 1919 while awaiting deletion. Deleted September 1919. No. 25r differed from other airships because her gas-bags were inserted and inflated after she was 'lifted' and before her keel was installed. Because of this she was subject to 'surging', because of the constant alteration of the centre of lift. She was used mostly as a training ship.

HMA R.26
Builder: Messrs Vickers
Length: 535 ft
Height: 75 ft
Diameter: 53 ft

Capacity: 943,000 cu ft, eighteen gas-bags
Engines: Four 250 hp Rolls-Royce engines
Top speed: 52 m.p.h.
Gross lift: 28.5 tons
Disposable lift: 6.5 tons
Structural details: as No. 23r, but was modified during building to incorporate all the alterations deemed necessary in light of experience gained by the previous three ships of this class, and had only one propeller on her rear car.

First flight 20 March 1918. Arrived Howden from Barrow 22 April 1918. Arrived Pulham 26 May 1918. Arrived Howden 31 May 1918. On 4/5 June 1918 made flight of 40 hours 40 minutes under the command of Capt T. Elmsley. Arrived Pulham 29 July 1918. On 25 October 1918 flew over London as part of the Lord Mayor's show, the only time an airship participated. On 20 November 1918, captained by Maj Watt, met surrendered German submarine fleet off Harwich, together with SR–1. On 21 and 22 January 1919 made two flights for National Physical Laboratory. Bows strengthened by diagonal wiring between frames 2 and 3 and used for mooring experiments with the three-wire system. She survived a week without harm but a bad snowstorm finally smashed her into the ground and she was broken up in situ on 24 February 1919. Hours flown: 191 hours 29 minutes 1918, 6 hours 18 minutes January 1919. Deleted 10 March 1919. In retrospect, R.26 can be seen as Britain's first truly operational rigid airship.

HMA R.27
Although basically the same as the '23' class ships, R.27 and R.29 became known as the '23x' class. They incorporated modifications instituted by Constructor-Commander Campbell on behalf of the Admiralty. The gas capacity was slightly increased by redesigning the bow and stern, but the great innovation was omitting the external keel. Campbell had discovered that a '23' class airship was strong enough without its keel, and that the fuel, ballast, bombs, etc., which were placed within the keel, could be distributed along the bottom two girders. Inverted U-shaped ribs on these bottom girders formed an internal walkway to all parts of the ship.

The aft car now contained a single engine with a propeller rather than the two engines and two swivelling propellers employed previously. R.27, along with R.29, was also given a modified fuel system, with a large diameter aluminium pipe running beneath the fuel tanks which could be used for filling or jettisoning fuel.

Builder: Messrs Beardmore
Length: 539 ft
Height: 75 ft
Diameter: 53 ft
Capacity: 990,000 cu ft
Engines: Four 300 hp Rolls-Royce engines
Top speed: 55 m.p.h.
Gross lift: 30.1 tons
Disposable lift: 8.5 tons

First flight 8 June 1918. Commissioned and trials at Inchinnan 29 June 1918. Flew immediately to her war station at Howden. On 10 August 1918, captained by Maj Ommaney, a flight of 23 hours 15 minutes. Hours flown 1918: 89 hours 40 minutes. Destroyed by fire in hangar at Howden after some US Navy crewmen assembled an extra un-numbered 'Zero' from the old envelope of SSZ.23 and an un-numbered car and engine. While wireless tests were being carried out, a spark ignited loose petrol. The conflagration engulfed this un-numbered 'Zero', R.27, SSZ.38 and SSZ.54 on 16 August 1918. Deleted Howden 16 August 1918.

HMA R.29
The Navy's first successful operational rigid airship, R.29 engaged three enemy U-boats.

No. 24r preparing for trials flight, Inchinnan, 27 October 1918. The rear car still has its engine and swivelling propellers. (Ces Mowthorpe Collection).

No. 25r landing after her maiden flight at Barlow, October 1917. (Ces Mowthorpe Collection)

R.26 landing after trials flight at Barrow, 20 March 1918. (Ces Mowthorpe Collection)

R.27 landing at Howden after her maiden flight, 29 June 1918. R.27 was the first of the 23X class; the external difference between her and her predecessor, R.26, can be seen clearly in this photograph. (Ces Mowthorpe Collection)

R.29 landing at East Fortune, July 1918. (Ces Mowthorpe Collection)

The first escaped, the second struck a mine while being pursued and the third, UB–115, was hit with a 220 lb bomb off the coast of Sunderland and finished off by destroyers called to the scene on 29 September 1918. Made flight of 32 hours 20 minutes on 3/4 July 1918. Broken up 24 October 1919 at East Fortune.

Builder: Messrs Armstrong-Whitworth
Length: 539 ft
Height: 75 ft
Diameter: 53 ft
Capacity: 990,000 cu ft, eighteen gas-bags
Engines: Four 300 hp Rolls-Royce engines
Top speed: 55 m.p.h.
Gross lift: 30.1 tons
Disposable lift: 8.5 tons
Structural details: as R.27

First flight 29 May 1918. Commissioned and made trials flight to Howden from Selby (Barlow) 20 June 1918. Arrived East Fortune 29 June 1918. Made two flights in July under Maj Thomas. W/T trials January 1919. Damaged while entering shed at East Fortune in May 1919. Amidships engine car changed to a smaller one containing only one engine driving its own propeller at the rear. In June 1919 made local flights over Edinburgh, Berwick and the Firth of Forth with R.34. Hours flown: 337 hours 25 minutes 1918, 100 hours 33 minutes 1919. Deleted 24 October 1919. Compared with R.26 she had a turning radius coefficient of 9.8 against the earlier ship's 11.2, i.e. she could turn about within a distance less than ten times her own length.

CHAPTER 10

POSTWAR AIRSHIPS

At the Armistice, British airships were still under Naval control, even though the RAF had been formed from the RFC and RNAS in April 1918. The airshipmen had fought valiantly for their country: casualties to RNAS airshipmen numbered 54 officers and men killed, and 175 officers and men had been injured. Five officers and men were missing, and another five officers and men had been interned.

Although it did not have as much expertise as the German Airship Branch in operating large rigids, the Navy was catching up fast and was ahead in non-rigid operations. Despite the great advances made with aeroplanes, it was still firmly believed that the future of intercontinental flying rested with the large airship.

In the immediate postwar period, Royal Naval airshipmen soon found themselves operating in unsettled conditions. Wartime contracts were run down, with production of the highly successful 'SS-Twin' class cut to thirteen from a three-figure number, and three of the 'North Sea' class were completed but never accepted. Nevertheless they made much progress: R.34 flew the Atlantic both ways in 1919; the mooring mast, both high and low-level, was to revolutionise airship handling; and new materials and advances in radio-navigation and weather forecasting were all attributable to the British airshipman. Regrettably it was all leading to a dead-end, but no-one could foresee the future that clearly.

R.31

At the end of the war, the large rigid airship programme included several airships in an advanced state of construction. The first of the two wooden-hulled rigids, R.31, had been accepted on 6 November 1918, having carried out her maiden flight in August. On her second flight the upper fin and rudder collapsed over the Home Counties. Fortunately these were secured by volunteers under Coxswain Cook (later the Tower Officer at Cardington), who was sent top-sides to secure the fin. He related that when the task was completed he looked down and they were over Reading, Berkshire. R.31 limped safely back to Cardington. Here the fins were re-attached and generally strengthened. With a capacity of 1,500,000 cu ft and a length of 615 ft, R.31 had a disposable lift of over 19 tons. Originally powered by six 300 hp Roll-Royce engines, she had attained a speed of over 70 m.p.h.; and 65 m.p.h. was still possible after one had been removed before acceptance.

On 6 November 1918 R.31 departed for Howden, en route to her war station at East Fortune. Although she arrived safely, minor repairs were carried out before she left on 12 November for East Fortune. Shortly after take-off a number of girders fractured in the hull so she returned to Howden. Housed in No. 1 shed where the R.27 catastrophe had occurred the previous August, leaks from its distorted roof damaged R.31's wooden framework so badly that R.31 was stripped and dismantled in situ during 1919. Her total flying time was recorded by the Navy as 4 hours 55 minutes.

R.32

R.31's sistership R.32 conducted her trials flight on 3 September 1919, then proceeded

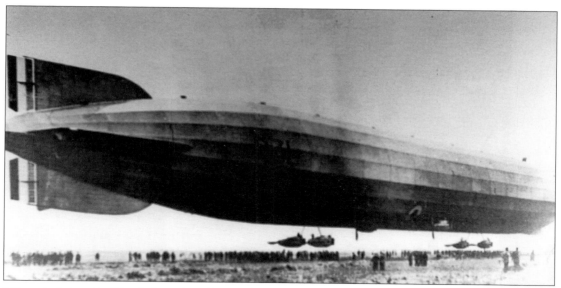

R.31 preparing for her maiden flight at Cardington, August 1918. Note that she has three pairs of engines. After her second flight – when her upper fin collapsed – one rear engine was dispensed with, the other repositioned on the centre-line. (Ces Mowthorpe Collection)

R.31, with the collapsed upper fin (see text), on her second trials flight, 16 October 1918. (Ces Mowthorpe Collection)

R.32 at Cardington. (Ces Mowthorpe Collection)

to Pulham. The delay in completing R.32 was simply due to 'peacetime working', a peculiar malady that afflicted the uncompleted ex-wartime rigids! Despite this delay – or perhaps because of it – R.32 was a successful and useful airship. Decommissioned when the RAF took over all airship operations from the Navy in October 1919, R.32 was immediately seconded to the National Physical Laboratory (NPL) for experiments on manoeuvring and parachuting. In March 1920, R.32 was at Howden training the American crew for their take-over of R.38, during which she flew 90 hours. A further 64 hours flying soon followed, including work with the NPL and the Americans. After approximately 250 flying hours, R.32 was broken up 'scientifically' by the NPL, which was conducting experiments on the strength of rigid airships.

One peculiarity of these two wooden airships was their flexibility in flight. Anyone standing in the control room doorway and watching a friend at the tail-end of the keel gangway would see him 'disappear' and then 'reappear' during turns!

R.33

Next came R.33 and R.34, two 'normal' metal ships. A length of 643 ft and diameter of 76 ft gave this class a capacity of 1,950,000 cu ft in nineteen gas-bags. Powered by five 240 hp Sunbeam Maori 4 engines, their maximum speed was 62 m.p.h. with a disposable lift of 26 tons. Both were almost identical copies of Zeppelin L.33, which had been brought down virtually intact at Little Wigborough on 24 September 1916.

R.33 was built by Messrs Armstrong Whitworth at Barlow in Yorkshire. (The fact that the British ship was numbered 33 is purely coincidental and has no connection with the number of the crashed Zeppelin.) After her trials flight at Barlow on 6 March 1919, R.33 flew directly to Pulham. Between then and 14 October, R.33 made 23 flights totalling 337 hours. By far Britain's most successful rigid, she had a number of memorable 'firsts'. A brass band played on her top gun platform during an extended flight extolling 'Victory Bonds'. Registered as a civil airship in April 1920, she carried the marks G-FAAB, performing numerous flights for the NPL and conducting extensive mooring trials at the Pulham high mast – on one occasion riding out gusts of up to 80 m.p.h. In May 1920 she released a pilotless Sopwith Camel over the North Yorkshire moors.

After overhaul at Howden, R.33 next checked out Croydon's night-flying lighting

R.33 in flight, Pulham, 1919. (Ces Mowthorpe Collection)

system, mooring to a specially-erected portable wooden mast. June 1921 then saw the ship assisting the police to monitor traffic at the Epsom races, and in July she appeared at the Hendon Air Pageant before next month flying to Cardington where she was shedded for over three years.

On 24 August 1921 the R.38 disaster put a stop to all British military airship development. Ships were struck off charge and scrapped. R.33 escaped this fate because she was now under civilian control, so when Ramsay MacDonald's Labour Government initiated an Airship Research Policy in 1924, plans were drawn up to resurrect R.33 to provide data for the proposed giant rigids R.100 and R.101. Thus on 2 April 1925 she again moored to the Cardington mast.

Completely reconditioned, with new modified gas-bags and engines, R.33 no longer carried RAF markings, only her registration letters in black on the hull and tail. Under complete civilian control (her crew were 'civilians', too), she at first made a number of short flights around Bedford – though still with her RAF bomb-release gear fitted!

After this relatively gentle start, R.33 suffered a perilous night on 16/17 April. While she was moored to the Pulham mast during a 50 m.p.h. gale, the mooring arm fractured. Out of control, R.33 narrowly missed the Pulham shed while the anchor-watch of eighteen men under Flt Lt Booth and Coxswain Hunt struggled to save their ship. With badly damaged bows and one gas-bag deflated, R.33 drifted stern-first across the North Sea. Eventually volunteers were able to secure the nose using the deflated gas-bag and lashings, and the engines were started and used to keep her head to wind. After 29 hours she made an almost triumphant return to Pulham, having crossed the North Sea and Dutch coastline. For his feat of airmanship Coxswain 'Sky' Hunt was awarded the AFM and each crewman received a gold watch from His Majesty King George V.

Repaired and fitted with a strengthened bow, R.33 spent October 1925 continuing with experimental work. She was fitted with a trapeze from which hung a De Havilland Hummingbird monoplane. Twice it was dropped but failed to reconnect in flight. Finally, on 4 December 1925, a successful 'hook-up' was achieved. Refitted, R.33 was then fitted with two connecting points for aeroplanes, and 26 October 1926 found her with two Gloster Grebe fighters suspended below the hull. Both were dropped successfully but no attempt was made to reconnect with them.

By now R.33 was showing signs of her age! Standing orders forbade more than four men standing together 'aft of Frame 33 at any one time' and 'There was to be no running in the keel'. A further pair of Gloster Grebes were dropped on 23 November 1926, plus two parachutists. Shedded at the end of November 1926, after 735 flying hours, severe 'fatigue' was discovered in her structure. Finally dismantled in 1928, the forward portion of her control car survives today in the RAF Museum at Hendon.

R.34

Identical in every way to R.33, R.34 was likewise to achieve fame. On 14 March 1919 she commenced her trials at Inchinnan, where a jammed elevator cable caused a heavy landing on her second flight. Repairs were undertaken before the Navy accepted her in late May 1919, when she was flown to her base at East Fortune. In company with R.29, she took part in a 6 hour flight around the Firth of Forth in June. This was followed by a 56 hour flight around the Baltic coast of northern Germany, fully armed, as part of a series of measures to 'persuade' the German Government to sign a peace treaty.

On 2 July 1919, R.34 began the first double crossing of the Atlantic by an aircraft. Landing at Mineola, Long Island, USA after 108 hours 12 minutes flying time, the crew were entertained like royalty. Nevertheless, moored to a three-wire system for three days, some anxious moments arose. When the mooring rope nearly broke free on the 8th, Capt Scott decided to leave the next day. The return crossing took only 75 hours 3 minutes as R.34 was assisted by the prevailing winds, and she landed safely at Pulham, where she had been diverted.

Returning to East Fortune, R.34 underwent a refit before returning to Pulham in February 1920. Permanently assigned to Howden in March 1920, she was then modified to take a mooring mast attachment, which was never fitted.

On 21 January 1921 R.34 left Howden on a trial flight after another refit, combining it with an exercise for eight trainee navigators. Due to a number of human errors, the ship was caught out in worsening weather over the North Yorkshire Moors. Lost, and trying to find a reference point, R.34 struck a hilltop on Guisborough Moor. Minor damage was done to the control car but both fore and aft propellers were smashed. This left only the two wing engines, on which, next day, she

R.34 in flight in 1919, just prior to her double crossing of the Atlantic in July 1919. (Ces Mowthorpe Collection)

struggled back to Howden. In a rising wind she landed with the aid of a 400-strong landing party, but they were unable to get her into her shed because of a strong crosswind.

During the night, moored out on the airfield on a three-wire system, she was pounded into the ground. In the morning it became clear the only option was to break her up on site and sell the remains for scrap: a sad demise for an excellent airship that had flown over 400 hours.

R.36

The last wartime ship to fly was the R.36, because R.35 was more or less completed by Armstrong-Whitworth but cancelled and 'reduced to scrap'. R.36 was designed using information from the wreckage of Zeppelin L.49 – which was brought down relatively intact at Bourbonne-les-Baines, France, in October 1917 – together with postwar knowledge gleaned from the Zeppelin company. Although work on the 'military' R.36 was suspended for a while, she was modified extensively and completed as a civilian ship, registered G-FAAF.

Built by Beardmore at Inchinnan, R.36 was 675 ft long with a diameter of 79 ft. This gave a capacity of 2,101,000 cu ft, producing a disposable lift of 16 tons. Beneath her hull was a 131 ft long passenger-car/control cabin, three 350 hp Sunbeam 'Cossack' and two 260 hp Maybach engines (from the dismantled Zeppelin L.71). This luxurious cabin contained fifty wicker chairs, tables, two-berth cabins, toilets and a galley. The Maybach engines, complete in their Zeppelin 'pods', were fitted well forward, port and starboard.

After a successful trial flight on 1 April 1921, R.36 next day flew to Pulham under the command of Flt Lt Wann. Three days later, while under the command of Maj Scott and carrying a number of Air Ministry officials and press correspondents, her upper fin and rudder collapsed. Only with skilful

piloting was she able to limp back to Pulham. The words of her navigating officer 'Tommy' Elmhirst tell the story:

'Off we went at 8 am on an April morning, with a reasonable weather report. Circling low over London we set course for Bath and Bristol. Scott gave me his intentions – "I shall work up to full power slowly, then give elevators and rudders a good testing." He personally supervised the testing of the controls, then left the control-car to go off to the dining-room to take part in the "Special Lunch" arranged for the passengers. His last instructions to me were "Keep her going at full speed for an hour and steady on this course at 4,000 ft." I suppose it was about twenty minutes after he had departed when disaster struck. Suddenly the ship went into a steep dive (I hung onto the side of the control-car and momentarily thought that this dive would put all the plates on the floor!). The height coxswain turned to me and said "Something wrong, Sir. I have lost control". Almost immediately the steering coxswain reported likewise.

'By now, R.36 was diving earthwards with all engines going at full power. Clawing my way to the engine telegraphs I rang "Stop engines", then stretched towards the water ballast tanks and let go half-a-ton of water from the ship's ballast-tank, hoping that this action would lift her bows level. Then down the ladder into the car came Scotty, quite calm and with a smile on his face, saying "Tommy, what on earth have you been doing to the ship?". Now all engines were stopped the dive slowly came to a halt with the ship starting to rise through use of the ballast.

'Scott was imperturbable. He said to me "Get into the keel and stand at the top of the ladder where you can take orders from me. Distribute the crew at each of the cross-sections in the keel then move them a section at a time, forward or aft, as I order." Then,

R.36 moored to the Pulham high mast. Note the civilian registration, G-FAAF, on the side. The two 260 hp Maybachs can be seen with their smaller cars in front of the 131 ft, fifty-seater passenger cabin, which has the control room at the front. (Ces Mowthorpe Collection)

by using a little power and moving the crew, control was regained, albeit only partially.

'Both coxswains were sent onto the top of the ship to report the damage, while we drifted like a balloon earthwards, rudderless – between Bath and Bristol. The coxswains reported that both vertical and horizontal tail-surfaces had either buckled or broken and it looked as if the whole tail might break off if too much power was applied. However, they thought they could disconnect the buckled elevator and rudder, secure them temporarily, then reconnect the lower rudder to the control and render it usable. (For this task, the riggers were deservedly awarded Air Force Medals.) Finally Scotty turned to me and said "Tommy, find a replacement then get below and set me a course for base – I can only give you 30 knots." We reached Pulham at dusk and Scott landed the ship perfectly using the movement of the crew in the keel as a "climb and dive" control.'

Repaired, R.36's short but eventful career was resumed as she helped police with the Ascot race traffic on 14 June 1921. On 27 June, forty-nine MPs had an hour's flight, returning to the new Cardington mast, which now had a lift. Then, on 21 June 1921, while mooring to the Pulham mast, the mooring rope fouled and the bow was badly damaged back to No. 2 frame. Because of impending bad weather, Zeppelin L.64 – brought to Pulham with L.71 as part of Germany's war reparations – was hastily broken up to make room for the damaged R.36. Even so, R.36 was further damaged while entering the shed and, although repaired, never flew again. Her flying time is recorded as 80 hours. She was deleted and broken up in 1926.

R.38

Of the remaining rigids under construction, R.37 was never fully completed. Built by Short Bros at Cardington, she was complete

R.38 about to be taken out of her shed at Cardington, 23 June 1921. Note the unfinished, and never to be completed, R.37 in the adjoining shed. (Ces Mowthorpe Collection)

except for her outer covering when she was cancelled and 'reduced to scrap'. Parts for her sistership, R.38, had been assembled by Short's at Cardington, while R.39 at Armstrong-Whitworth's Barlow works was in a similar state to R.37. Meanwhile orders for R.40 and R.41 had been given to Beardmore or Armstrong-Whitworth, depending whose berths became available first. In the run-down of the airship service after the Armistice, work on these rigids was continued on a gradually reducing scale. Although these 'post-wartime' airships, referred to in Admiralty papers as the 'A-class' and 'the 40-class', incorporated all the latest developments gleaned from Zeppelins and other sources, none ever flew.

The British rigid programme was saved by the USA's wish to order a large rigid airship. As the Zeppelin works were at this time prevented by the Allies from selling airships, only Britain could oblige. The Admiralty literally turned Short Bros out of its Cardington site, offering minimum financial settlement, and Cardington became the Royal Airship Works (RAW) under Constructor-Commander Campbell. Cdr Campbell had a major problem. The American specification was complex, with long-range, low-level and high-level requirements. It was obvious the airship was going to be the largest yet produced by Britain and yet the Cardington shed was only 700 ft long. This restricted the RAW's options and so influenced the design significantly.

The resulting design was 699 ft long, 86 ft wide and 95 ft high, with a capacity of 2,724,000 cu ft and a disposable lift of 45.6 tons. She was powered by six 350 hp Sunbeam Cossack engines in individual cars and had a design speed of 70.6 m.p.h. Meanwhile, the airship numbering system was 'adjusted'! This airship was allotted the designation R.38 and, indeed, a few of the

R.38 leaving her Cardington shed for the first time, 23 June 1921. (Ces Mowthorpe Collection)

original R.38's (and R.40's) parts were incorporated!

The new R.38's maiden flight took place on the night of 23/24 June 1921 and she remained airborne for 7 hours, during which time a number of faults developed. The airship was re-shedded and put in order. The second flight took place on the night of 28/29 June, and again serious problems arose, so further remedial work was carried out. Her third and final flight from Cardington took place on the night of 16/17 July, landing at Howden. This flight showed up yet more snags, especially her behaviour at speed, believed to be caused by over-balanced elevators.

Meanwhile a controversy arose about R.38's testing period. Suggestions were put forward for long-term trials of up to 50 flights, including ones in bad weather. However, the American crew that had trained at Howden were ready to fly the airship back to the USA, and they were getting impatient. The Air Ministry, too, wanted rid of R.38, in order to 'get the money' and hopefully attract additional orders! It was finally agreed that after the fourth (presumably trouble-free) test flight, R.38 would be handed over to the American crew who would moor to the Pulham mast before preparing to fly to the USA.

Meanwhile, at Howden, R.38 had been undergoing further alterations and was repainted in her American markings as ZR–2. At last, on 23 August 1921, the airship left Howden for the Pulham mast with a mixed crew of 49 (including 16 Americans). During the night the ship cruised down the East Coast carrying out various tests, and morning found them near a fog-bound Pulham. Eventually, ordered back to Howden, they re-traced their course.

As the ship had flown only in calm weather, it is believed that the captain, Flt Lt Wann, was persuaded to simulate turbulent conditions by inducing violent alterations of course while at speed.

At 17.27 hours GMT, R.38 was seen to break up in mid-air south of Hull, over the River Humber. The tail section floated safely into the river but two explosions blew apart the fore section. There were five survivors, including Flt Lt Wann who was in the control cabin.

As a result of this tragedy, all military airship development in Britain was stopped.

R.80

The last of the wartime rigids was numbered completely out of sequence. This was R.80, built by Vickers to the Admiralty's November 1917 specification. At this time the new Vickers Airship Works at Flookburgh in Lancashire was still under construction, so an order for a '33' class airship could not be entertained because the Vickers shed at Barrow was too small.

Perhaps it was for this reason that Barnes Wallis was given a free hand to design his own airship. (Due to problems with the site, the Flookburgh works was never completed.)

R.80 had a capacity of 1,200,000 cu ft in a perfectly streamlined hull 535 ft long and 70 ft wide. She was fitted with four 230 hp Wolseley-Maybach engines, two in a double installation driving a single propeller behind the control car and two in single streamlined power cars amidships. These gave her a top speed of 60 m.p.h with a disposable lift of 17.8 tons.

Everything about R.80 was practical. For example, all of her wiring was colour-coded, and her streamlining was excellent. There is little doubt she could have proved the finest British rigid if she had become fully operational – equal to contemporary Zeppelins! Yet because of alterations specified by the Admiralty and the end of hostilities, her maiden flight did not take place until 19 July 1920. It was nearly

R.80 taking off from Howden, spring 1921. (Ces Mowthorpe Collection)

disastrous. She was left standing for several hours in full sun, which superheated the gas. As a result, she went out of control during the initial climb, shooting up to over 4,000 ft and breaking several girders.

As a result, her second flight was not undertaken until January 1921. During repairs, she was fitted with bow mooring gear, plus a ton of ballast to the stern to compensate! These proved no problem as she had a gross lift of more than 2 tons above specification. On 24 February 1921 she left for Howden, and on arrival was immediately deflated as the airship programme was run down.

The loss of R.34 produced a reprieve for R.80, because the American crew being trained to fly R.38 demanded a 'metal' ship instead of the wooden R.32. Between 26 March and 1 June 1921 R.80 made at least four training flights totalling 8 hours 43 minutes. Her final flight was to Pulham under

Flt Lt Booth – carrying 'the CO's livestock' to his new post! R.80's total flying time is recorded as 75 hours.

R.80 remained intact until 1923 when she was tested 'scientifically to destruction'.

THE VICKERS 'PARSEVAL'
During 1920 Messrs Vickers received an order for a Parseval-type airship, complete with mooring mast, from the Japanese Navy. This ship, which became Naval Airship No. 1 of the Japanese Imperial Navy, was 170 ft long, 38 ft wide and 50 ft high, with a capacity of 100,000 cu ft. Its car was a streamlined version of the Vickers-built P.6 and P.7 car; powered by two 100 hp Sunbeam Dyak engines, its speed was 60 m.p.h. Several trial flights took place at Barrow, starting on 27 April 1921, and the ship was moored to the accompanying Masterman Mast for a short period.

[The Masterman Mast was the brain-child

The Vickers 'Parseval' secured to the Masterman Mast in the Vickers Walney island shed, 1921. This ship became Naval Airship No. 1 of the Japanese Imperial Navy. (Brian Turpin)

of E.A.D. Masterman, Capt Scott and Vickers. Designed specially for non-rigids, the top of the mast was forked, each curved 'prong' resting against a special pad built into an airship's envelope. Although tested and developed, it never saw operational use.] However, one was supplied to Japan with the airship. On 10 July 1922 the ship caught fire in its shed and was totally destroyed.

AD–1 – THE ADVERTISING AIRSHIP

Some years were to elapse before 1929 found Capt Weir-MacCall AFC, J.R. Pike and Engineer R.H. Schlotel designing a small non-rigid airship to be used commercially as an advertising medium. Appropriately named AD–1, it had a modest capacity of 60,000 cu ft and supported a two-seat car containing a 75 hp ABC Hornet engine mounted in the nose. Piloted by Capt MacCall, who was accompanied by ex-RNAS Coxswain Jerry Long, the new ship made her maiden flight at her Cramlington base, near Newcastle, on 2

September 1929, and four further flights on 18 September 1929. Capt MacCall then departed the company and his place was taken by Capt 'Bingo' Beckford Ball who carried out more flying on 18 October and 6 and 29 November 1929.

During the Challenge and Grosvoner meeting at Cramlington Airfield on 5 October 1929, AD–1 flew around the field with a large notice each side pronouncing 'this space to let'. In November, Capt Meager carried out the necessary CAA test flight, before it was deflated in December for modifications.

Re-inflated in May 1930, in June AD–1 advertised 'WILSON'S FINE FOODS' before departing Cramlington for Grantham on 21 June, then flying on to Capel on 26 June 1930. She reached East Horsley on 17 July and made two flights over London. During August, her engine was changed to a 75 hp Rolls-Royce Hawk, and her propeller broke and punctured the envelope. On 16

AD–1 at Cramlington ex-airship station, Northumberland, 13 September 1929. (Ces Mowthorpe Collection)

September 1930 she was flown across Channel to Ostend advertising 'GOLD DOLLAR CIGARETTES'. Moored out at Ichteghen, AD–1 was wrecked by a storm on 7 October 1930. Her company was wound up on the 11th whereupon she was auctioned. In a sad end, her engine was sold for £20 and her envelope for £12 10s (£12.50).

R.100

In 1924 the Labour Government under Ramsay MacDonald initiated an airship research programme to study the practicability of large rigid airships flying routes throughout the Empire. Similar ventures had been proposed by private companies, but none had borne fruit because there were no airships large enough to be competitive.

The government's programme allocated £1,350,000, spread over three years, for the construction of two large commercially operated rigids and for setting up three bases in Canada, Egypt and India. R.33 would be recommissioned to assist this programme. With the R.38 tragedy in mind, both airships would be scientifically checked and tested.

It was decided that the Air Ministry would construct one of the airships and the other would be built by private enterprise. This would make for healthy competition!

Briefly, the specification for these two giants was a capacity of 5,000,000 cu ft and a 'useful' lift of 50 tons. They should have full living accommodation for 100 passengers, and be capable of carrying them at a cruising speed of 63 m.p.h. and a top speed of 70 m.p.h.

Sisterships in specification and appearance they might have been, but they did in fact differ considerably. The 'private' contract, designated R.100, was awarded to the Airship Guarantee Company, a subsidiary of Vickers. The design team moved to the ex-RNAS station at Howden, where the huge double shed was renovated, gas-plant installed and accommodation provided. In charge was Sir Dennis Burney, with Barnes-Wallis as his chief designer and Neville Shute Norway (better known as Neville Shute, the author) the chief calculator.

At this time, the leading rigid airships, the Zeppelins, had a central wire running from the nose cone to the tail cone, through the gas-bags. Onto this was attached a 'slack-wire' system in the middle of each frame. Barnes-Wallis went one better! He substituted a central girder instead of a wire. Barnes Wallis also perfected a system of constructing the girders using helically-wound duralumin strip, lapped and riveted. As a result, R.100 was one of the strongest airships ever built.

As built, R.100 had a total capacity of 5,156,000 cu ft and a length of 709 ft. Originally it was intended to install diesel engines, but these failed to reach their specified power, and so Barnes Wallis was permitted to substitute six ex-RAF factory-reconditioned 660 hp Rolls-Royce Condor IIIB engines. These were installed in three tandem engine cars, with each rear engine being reversible. The control car projected below the hull in the normal fashion, but the entire passenger and crew accommodation was grouped into three 'floors' suspended internally, with large windows in the lower hull.

On 16 December 1929, R.100 made her maiden flight from her birthplace to the Cardington mast, and a second flight on the following day. On 11 January 1930 she made her third flight, a 14 hour trip around southern England, then carried 60 people over London on 20 January, before undertaking a 35 hour flight on 27–29 January 1930.

During these flights, various tests were being made on the airship, and then R.100 was shedded at Cardington while

R.100 at Howden prior to her maiden flight to Cramlington, 16 December 1929. This photograph shows up R.100's perfect proportions, which were marred somewhat when her tail cone fractured during a flight on 22 May 1930. It was not replaced, and a 'plug' was inserted leaving a blunt tail. (Ces Mowthorpe Collection)

modifications were put in hand and preparations made for a flight to Canada.

Flight number six was on 21 May 1930, with 65 people on board for a 22 hour session. On R.100's return to the Cardington mast, Flying Officer Cook, the officer-in-charge of the tower (mooring-mast), radioed to say that her tail cone was hanging down! R.100 was shedded immediately, and the previous tail 'point', aft of the fins, was plugged with a solid material and covered over. Barnes-Wallis was extremely annoyed that the fairing was not replaced and resented the 'ugly plug' that marred R.100's beautiful symmetry – he had an artist's appreciation which showed in all his work.

At the same time a water-recovery system, the brain-child of Chief Coxswain T.E. Greenstreet, was fitted to the outside of the envelope. So successful was this system that R.101 incorporated it, as did the German *Graf Zeppelin*. Flying was resumed on 25 July 1930 with the ship airborne for 24 hours testing direction-finding and radio equipment.

At 02.48 hours on 29 July 1930 she finally commenced her trans-Atlantic flight. All went well until R.100 was nearing Quebec, where the ship was struck by a 'white squall' – known today as severe turbulence. Fortunately she suffered only torn fabric on the control surfaces, and it was possible to carry out temporary repairs in flight with the ship stationary at 1,500 ft.

Near Montreal another squall upset a tin of dope, which necessitated all electrics being shut down because of its inflammable nature. Finally, R.100 secured to the Montreal mast after a flight of 78 hours 49 minutes, having covered 3,364 nautical miles and consumed 29.5 tons of fuel.

While in Canada, R.100 made a 25 hour

37 minute flight around the Eastern Counties and Niagara Falls, with representatives of the Canadian Services aboard. During this flight the reduction-gear on the forward starboard engine burst. As this could not be repaired, she had to make the return journey across the Atlantic on five engines.

On 14 August 1930, R.100 left Montreal mast and set course for Cardington, with 56 personnel aboard. Arriving there on 16 August after a 57 hour 36 minute flight of 2,935 nautical miles, she was shedded and never flew again. When R.101 crashed at Beauvais in October, the airship programme was axed and Barnes-Wallis' great airship was reduced to scrap and sold.

R.101

Like her sistership, R.101 was the result of the 1924 airship research programme and was built by the government at the Royal Airship Works at Cardington. Being the 'government ship', R.101 always received the greater publicity. Her design team consisted of Col Vincent Richmond, an able engineer specialising in rigid airships, and his assistant, Sqn Ldr Rope, a highly respected lighter-than-air engineering officer.

From the start this ship was wholly experimental. She incorporated many innovations which, although laudable, had never been tried previously. The entire framework was made of stainless steel. Fabricated by Messrs Boulton & Paul of Norwich, it was machined to tolerances of .015 in 10 ft and .030 inches in 30 ft and fitted together like a giant Meccano set.

R.101 was powered by five 600 hp Beardmore Tornado diesel engines, each in its own 'power egg' suspended below the hull. All of the engines were pushers, with a cable passing through each propeller-boss and secured to a main-frame aft in order to anchor their powerful thrust.

Although they were intended for reversible-thrust propellers, which were never fitted, none of the engines were reversible themselves. As a temporary measure, the aft

R.101 at Cardington mast, as first flown in October 1929. (Ces Mowthorpe Collection)

engine on the centre-line was fitted with a reversible-pitch propeller and used only for manoeuvring at the mast! On her final flight, to India, these engines carried normal wooden propellers, the two forward ones having variable valve-timing which allowed them to be stopped, then restarted in reverse.

R.101's passenger accommodation was even more luxurious than R.100's. Although a small control car projected beneath the hull, everything else was accommodated inside on two decks that, unlike the 'free suspension' system of R.100, were an integral part of the frame. The luxurious passenger accommodation consisted of a 160 ft × 30 ft lounge with imitation palm-trees, wicker chairs and tables, promenade decks and cabins. There was even circulating hot air for warmth. Officer and crew accommodation was on the smaller second deck. (The luxury went only so far – curtains were used as doors to save weight.)

It should be remembered that both these huge airships were experimental. But where Barnes-Wallis had followed a traditional path, the Cardington team were reaching out to the ends of technology. It is not surprising therefore that R.101 suffered problems from the start. The outer covers of both R.100 and R.101 gave trouble, but R.101 had been 'pre-doped'. This set up a chemical reaction and every bit of the amidships section had to be cleaned and renewed.

Also, R.101's initial static tests found that she could lift only 35 tons. As this was unacceptable, all excess weight – servo-motors, the look-out cockpits, etc. – was removed, and celluloid replaced the heavier glass. To gain extra lift, the gas-bags were expanded to their farthest limits. This gas-bag system was unique. Invented by Sqn Ldr Rope, it consisted of a special harness for each cell; if properly used, it may have been an excellent innovation. Unfortunately, the extending cells now rubbed against the framework, causing constant leaks and a need for much patching.

These measures gained an extra 9 tons of

R.101 at Cardington mast in October 1930 after a 45 ft bay had been installed, aft of the control car. The airship was now 777 ft long, and had an increased volume of 5,509,753 cu ft. (Ces Mowthorpe Collection)

lift. It was then decided to cut R.101 in two and insert a further bay and gas-bag, in order to gain another 9 tons of lift. The insertion of an extra bay – a quite normal practice with the Zeppelins – gave R.101 a final overall length of 777 ft, 44 ft longer than first constructed.

Testing to destruction of a special section of R.101's frame delayed construction proper until April 1927. Altogether, eleven flights were carried out, all in good weather. Even so, R.101 was not a stable airship, rolling in the horizontal plane and hunting in the vertical plane.

The twelfth and final fight to India was imposed on R.101 for political reasons. Tragically she set off on the evening of 4 October 1930, her Certificate of Airworthiness being handed to the captain only minutes before departure. At 02.00 hours she struck a hill at Beauvais, France and burst into flames. There were only four survivors.

Should any reader wish for more details of R.101, several excellent books have been written about her. Two worthy of perusal are

To Ride The Storm by Sir Peter Masefield and *The Millionth Chance* by James Leason.

POST-SECOND WORLD WAR DEVELOPMENTS

In Britain, all airship development ceased after the loss of R.101, and it was not until after the Second World War that further airship flights took place.

In 1948 Lord Ventry founded the Airship Club to raise funds and design and build a small airship. A number of ex-airshipmen including Sqn Ldr T.P. York-Moore, Gerry Long, Freddie Twinn, rigger Ralph Deverell and engineers Arthur Bell and Joe Binks became involved.

The new airship's envelope was modified from an ex-French kite balloon. Its control car was built by Alex Leith and assembled at Hurn airport during spring 1951, before being taken to Cardington for assembly. Suspension was the work of L.A. Speed, and a Flt Lt A. Richardson assisted in putting together the car and envelope. With a capacity of 45,000 cu ft, length of 108 ft and diameter of 28 ft, it attained a speed of 27

Bournemouth at Cardington, prior to her first flight, 19 July 1951. The pilot was Jack Beckford-Ball. (Ces Mowthorpe Collection)

m.p.h. driven by a Samson engine with pusher propeller.

After final trim tests on July 1951, it was first flown by Pilot Beckford-Ball at Cardington in 1951. The venture had only been possible through Lord Ventry's home town of Bournemouth providing some money as part of the Festival of Britain in 1951, so on 28 August this small airship was registered G-AMJH and named *Bournemouth*. It could carry a pilot and three passengers, but there were problems with the stability, so in 1952 her tail surfaces were redesigned by De Havilland's E.J. Mann, and these proved highly successful. Meanwhile an old bus was obtained and fitted with a stub mast, which enabled *Bournemouth* to enter and leave Cardington's No. 2 shed very easily.

During August and September 1952 a number of flights took place including several flights around Bournemouth during that town's Battle of Britain celebrations. Re-inflated in 1953, some netting slipped onto her envelope and damaged it beyond repair.

THE CHITTY-CHITTY-BANG-BANG AIRSHIP

In 1967 a miniature 'Lebaudy Airship' was built for the film *Chitty-Chitty-Bang-Bang*. Some 140 ft long, 50 ft high and with a

A replica of a Lebaudy airship, built in 1967, not to scale, for the film *Chitty-Chitty-Bang-Bang*. The pilots were D. Piggott and M. Brighton, but the ship flew only three or four times. (Ces Mowthorpe Collection)

capacity of 37,000 cu ft, it had a car containing two pilots and a modified Volkswagen 40 hp engine belt-driving two propellers. Pilot Derek Piggot operated the elevators and rudders, while Pilot Malcolm Brighton operated throttle, gas and ballast!

Proving unstable, she made only a few local test flights. Finally the ship hit some power cables, making a 'ripped' landing, luckily without damage to the occupants. A larger envelope was then made and the ship re-rigged. Unfortunately a freak gale destroyed her at her moorings before she could again be flown. This ill-fated airship was mostly moored in a clearing, in a valley near Turnville, Marlow, Buckinghamshire.

THE 'SANTOS-DUMONT'

Between 1974 and 1976 a group of enthusiasts, including the pilots, Anthony Smith and Jasper Tomlinson, built and flew a small airship at Cardington. Some 72 ft long with a diameter of 38 ft, it had a capacity of 30,000 cu ft. Power was provided by two 20 hp Wankel Rotary-valve engines, each driving a small ducted propeller. A pilot and two passengers sat in the very basic car. With fuel for four hours flying, a maximum speed of 30 knots was attained.

Registered G-BAWL and inflated with hydrogen (at a cost of £200), this little airship – sometimes known as the 'Santos-Dumont' – had a few teething troubles, but these were soon eliminated. The first flights took place at Cardington in 1974. Re-inflated with hydrogen again in 1975, further short flights were carried out, mostly in the early morning or evening, in still air.

During 1975 the firm of Gas & Equipment donated the cost of an envelope of helium (worth about £2,000), so CAA approval was

The 'Santos-Dumont', Cardington, 12 August 1975. This ship flew during the summers of 1973, '74 and '75. (Ces Mowthorpe Collection)

sought in 1976. Prior to this being granted, G-BAWL was unavoidably driven into some trees after a visit to nearby Old Warden, causing serious damage to the envelope. A whip-round among the crowd, who saw this incident, enabled enough helium to be 'hired' for the CAA examiner to complete his successful examination with a 1 hour 20 minute flight. Regrettably, after the 1976 season, this gallant venture into airships apparently ceased to exist.

CONCLUSION

The story of traditional 'canvas and string' British airships must end with the 'Santos-Dumont' ship. Nevertheless, from 1972 the American Goodyear airship *Europa* has graced the skies of this sceptred isle, between visits to the Continent, and Roger Munk's brilliant AD.500 – prototype for the later Skyship-600 series – first flew in the early 1980s at Cardington. A truly fine British venture.

These modern technological marvels cannot be compared with the relatively simple 'battlebags' of earlier days. For that reason alone, they are not included here. It must never be forgotten that the pioneers – many of them wartime Royal Naval personnel – carried out duties and overcame the unknown with simple common sense, shared experiences and discipline. Their legacy is today's worldwide airline system.

APPENDIX A

ROYAL NAVY NUMBERING

This appendix lists Royal Naval numbering of British airships from June 1914 (when the RN assumed responsibility for all lighter-than-air craft) and its continuation with the RAF and the two civil airships from the Royal Airship Works, Cardington.

When the Royal Naval Air Service was formed on 23 June 1914 it took control of all the services' airships. True to Naval fashion it classified them, as rigids, semi-rigids and non-rigids, built or on order. The airships were numbered in a proper numerical manner. Nos. 11, 12 and 13 were three Italian Forlaninis which were never delivered. Nos. 21 and 22 were the Kingsnorth designs, *Epsilon 1* and 2; work on these was stopped in late 1914, and they were never completed. All rigids had the suffix 'r' until No. 26.

From then they were prefixed by the capital letter 'R', e.g. R.26.

Thus, until R.34, a logical numbering system operated, bearing in mind that R.28 and R.30 were not built because new designs had taken over from the '23x' class. Likewise R.35, R.37 and R.40 were cancelled – even though the first two had almost been completed – due to the Armistice. When the two large civil airships were numbered in the later 1920s, they became R.100 and R.101 – perhaps it was deemed necessary to have a fresh start at 100 for civil craft! A little known fact is that the Royal Airship Works at Cardington had started work on the successor of R.101 – numbered R.102 – when all airship operations were halted by the crash of R.101 at Beauvais, France, on 4 October 1930.

Number	Name	Maker
1r	*Mayfly (Hermione)*	Vickers, Barrow
2		Willows No. 4
3		Astra-Torres
4		Parseval
5		Vickers, Barrow (Parseval)
6		Vickers, Barrow (Parseval)
7		Vickers, Barrow (Parseval)
8		Astra-Torres
9r		Vickers, Barrow
10		Astra-Torres
11		Forlanini (undelivered)
12		Forlanini (undelivered)
13		Forlanini (undelivered)
14r		Armstrong-Whitworth (cancelled)
15r		Armstrong-Whitworth (cancelled)

Number	Name	Maker
16		Astra-Torres
17	*Beta*	Farnborough
18	*Gamma*	Farnborough
19	*Delta*	Farnborough
20	*Eta*	Farnborough
21	*Epsilon 1*	Kingsnorth (cancelled)
22	*Epsilon 2*	Kingsnorth (cancelled)
23r		Vickers, Barrow
24r		Beardmore, Inchinnan
25r		Armstrong-Whitworth, Barlow
R.26		Vickers, Barrow
R.27		Beardmore, Inchinnan
R.28		Beardmore and Vickers (cancelled)
R.29		Armstrong-Whitworth, Barlow
R.30		Armstrong-Whitworth (cancelled)
R.31		Short Bros, Cardington
R.32		Short Bros, Cardington
R.33		Armstrong-Whitworth, Barlow
R.34		Beardmore, Inchinnan
R.35		Armstrong-Whitworth (cancelled)
R.36		Beardmore, Inchinnan
R.37		Short Bros, Cardington (cancelled)
R.38		Short Bros, later Royal Airship Works, Cardington
R.39		Armstrong-Whitworth (cancelled)
R.40		Short Bros, Cardington (cancelled)
R.41		Armstrong-Whitworth or Beardmore (cancelled)
R.80		Vickers, Barrow
R.81		Vickers (contract never signed)
R.100		Vickers Airship Guarantee Co, Howden
R.101		Royal Airship Works, Cardington
R.102		Royal Airship Works design

CONSTRUCTIONAL DETAILS AND DRAWINGS

One result of the Zeppelin raids on Great Britain during early 1915 was two meetings of the Admiralty, in June and July of that year. These meetings decreed that a rigid airship building programme should be embarked upon. No. 9r, Britain's second rigid airship, had in fact been started (No. 1r, 'Mayfly', was the first), but work on her had been suspended in favour of non-rigid ships and aeroplanes at the outbreak of war.

The order for work on No. 9r to recommence was promptly given. In order to speed up production of four similar rigids, the design was modified by increasing the fullness of the bow and stern and the insertion of another gas-bag to give improved lift. Then another engine car was added to improve performance. As Vickers possessed

Erection of a shed at the Armstrong-Whitworth Works, Barlow, near Selby, 1916. No. 25, R.29 and R.33 were built here. (Ces Mowthorpe Collection)

the only shed for building rigid airships, at Walney Island, Barrow-in-Furness, the modified design had to fit into it! The new type became known as the '23' class.

Subsequently, Messrs Armstrong-Whitworth and Beardmore were given the orders for '23' class rigids. They built double sheds at Barlow, Yorkshire (Armstrong-Whitworth) and Inchinnan (Beardmore). These were 700 ft long, 150 ft wide and 100 ft high, and each was capable of containing two rigid airships side by side. These became known as 'rigid constructional sheds', together with the later Shorts Brothers 700 ft × 180 ft × 110 ft sheds at Bedford and existing Vickers 539 ft × 148 ft × 97 ft sheds at Walney Island.

A shortage of steel for the war effort caused the Admiralty to argue against rigid airships, because each shed contained enough steel to build a light cruiser! However, the argument that a cruiser might be torpedoed and lost finally won the day!

At Barlow, Armstrong-Whitworth built No. 25r, R.29 and R.33. R.35 was virtually completed in 1919 but cancelled and scrapped because of the Armistice. At Inchinnan, Beardmore built No. 24r, R.27, R.34 and R.36, while Vickers built No. 9r, No. 23r, R.26 and R.80. The latter company was erecting a large constructional shed at Flookburgh but, owing to problems with the foundations, this was never completed. However, it was Vickers that designed the '23' class and manufactured most of the steelwork. This was transported by rail and assembled at Barlow and Inchinnan. Vickers also manufactured the gas-cells for rigids and gas-bags for non-rigids.

It was Messrs Short Bros which built the constructional shed at Cardington near Bedford – later to be taken over by the Government and named the Royal Airship Works – where the two wooden-hulled rigids, R.31 and R.32, were constructed. R.37, a metal ship, was completely assembled there by 1919, but it was never inflated or flown. R.37 was eventually scrapped. After the Admiralty took over Cardington in 1919, R.38 was built there for the American Navy as ZR–2.

At the outbreak of the war, another constructional shed was built at Barking, Essex. This was part of an isolated attempt at building rigid airships and had a peculiar history.

Before 1914, Britain had seen the Zeppelin as a real threat. No aeroplane could equal a Zeppelin's performance, so it was thought the only way to stop these huge craft was to attack them using a similar airship, known at the time as a 'killer airship'. For a time, fleets of such airships were envisaged, fighting for the control of the skies in a manner of the world's navies!

Naturally, such schemes fell by the wayside as the performance of the aeroplane increased. However, such a 'killer airship' was constructed, but not flown, in Britain. It was known by several names, e.g. the Macmchen Airship, the Macmechan Zeppelin Destroyer or the Marshall-Fox Airship, to name but three.

Extreme secrecy surrounded the building by Marshall-Fox of a large shed at Barking, near London. T.R. Macmechan was a journalist who became President of the Aeronautical Society of America. The designer, Walter K. Kamp, took patents out in America and Britain for this airship. With a length of 236 ft, a diameter of 28 ft and a capacity of about 108,000 cu ft, it was supposed to have range of 300 miles, a speed of 50 m.p.h. and carry a crew of four plus their 'armament'. It was powered by two engines, a 75 hp Green and a 125 hp ENV, which drove four propellers by direct cable drive. Also incorporated was an unusual technique of heating the hydrogen to increase lift and cool it to descend, using engine exhaust gases.

The whole 'killer airship' concept was

flawed. Nevertheless, it received some official backing. Five airships were proposed and the writer has evidence that several well-known aeronautical people were involved. Thus a shed, 266 ft long, 50 ft wide and 60 ft high, was constructed at Barking in May 1915. Rails were laid out from the entrance, and electric winches were provided to assist a ship's entry and exit.

Airship construction commenced immediately. The craft's rigid frame was made of wood, using a principle similar to the early German Shutte-Lanz airships. Two ENV engines were delivered and at least one fitted to the propeller-drive and tested. Late in June 1916, the Admiralty took over the 'Marshall-Fox Establishment' at Barking and nothing further was heard.

Speaking to an elderly resident of Barking, some years ago, I discovered that this shed was carefully guarded and supposed to contain a 'secret weapon'! Later on, towards the end of the war, the whole project was presumed to be something of a swindle, as nothing ever came from it. The shed survived for a number of years after the war.

When the postwar civil airship scheme got under way in 1924, the 'civil' R.100, built by Vickers, was constructed in the huge double shed of the wartime Howden station in Yorkshire. Meanwhile, the Cardington shed was enlarged, and the large Pulham shed dismantled and shipped to Cardington, where it too was enlarged. Thus, in 1924, Cardington became the Royal Airship Works and R.101 was built there.

RNAS Kingsnorth had two constructional sheds, 555 ft × 109 ft × 100 ft, and 700 ft × 150 ft × 98 ft. Both these sheds were used only for building non-rigids. Following the building of *Eta*, Farnborough designed another non-rigid airship designated *Epsilon*. Certainly the design was near completion because it was continued at RNAS Kingsnorth, where it was intended to build two of this class. When the Admiralty officially numbered its airships in June 1914, *Epsilon 1* and *Epsilon 2* became HMA.21 and HMA.22 respectively.

Neither was completed. However, in the Public Record Office at Kew there are some engineering drawings of details, plus one simple general arrangement, which show an ordinary streamlined circular-section envelope with an indicated capacity of 230,000 cu ft. The car shown is obviously an outline sketch but appears similar to the *Eta* car/gondola, only larger. The engines are given as Austro-Daimlers of 120 hp. These drawings are dated, variously, October, November and December 1913.

Last but not least, RNAS Wormwood Scrubs had a constructional shed of 354 ft × 75.5 ft × 98 ft. Like Kingsnorth, it built only non-rigids.

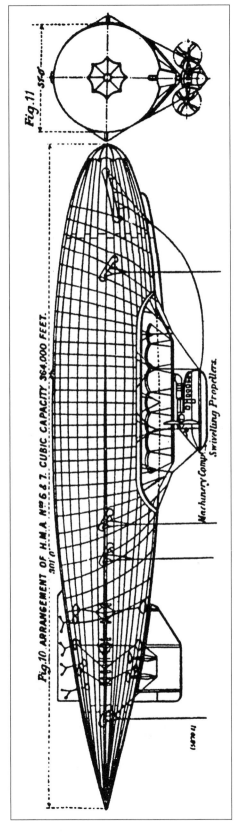

Fig.11

Fig.10 APPARATUS OF H.M.A. Nos 6 & 7. CUBIC CAPACITY 364,000 FEET.

Machinery Comp.

Swivelling Propellers.

Parseval P.6 and P.7.

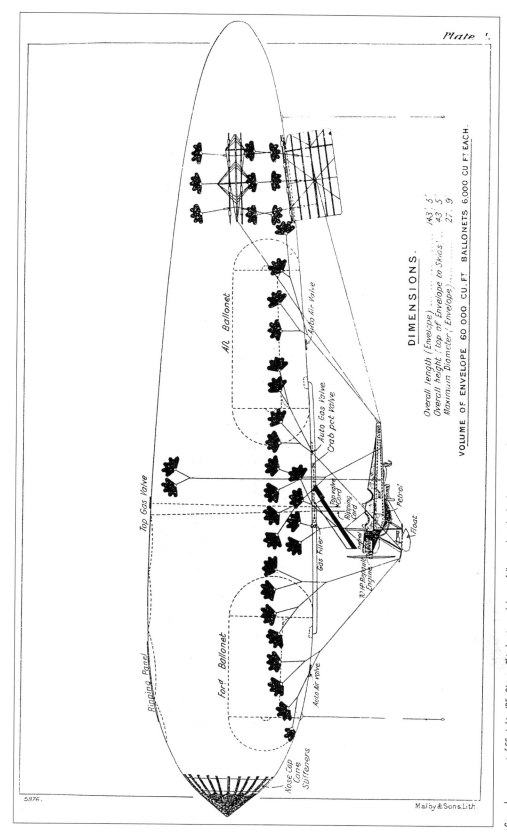

Plate 1.

Nose Cap Cane Stiffeners

Ripping Panel

Ford Ballonet

Auto Air valve

Top Gas Valve

Aft Ballonet

Auto Air Valve

Auto Gas Valve
Crab pot valve

Gas Filler

Top valve Kord
Ripping Cord

Petrol

Petrol

Float

70 H.P. Renault Engine

DIMENSIONS.

Overall length (Envelope) .... 143'. 5'
Overall height : top of Envelope to Skids ... 43'. 5'
Maximum Diameter : Envelope) .... 27'. 9

VOLUME OF ENVELOPE 60 000 CU.FT BALLONETS 6,000 CU.FT EACH.

5876.

Malby & Sons, Lith.

General arrangement of SS airship, 'BE–2' type. This drawing and the two following show the distributive pattern of 'Eta' patches.

Plate XXXI.

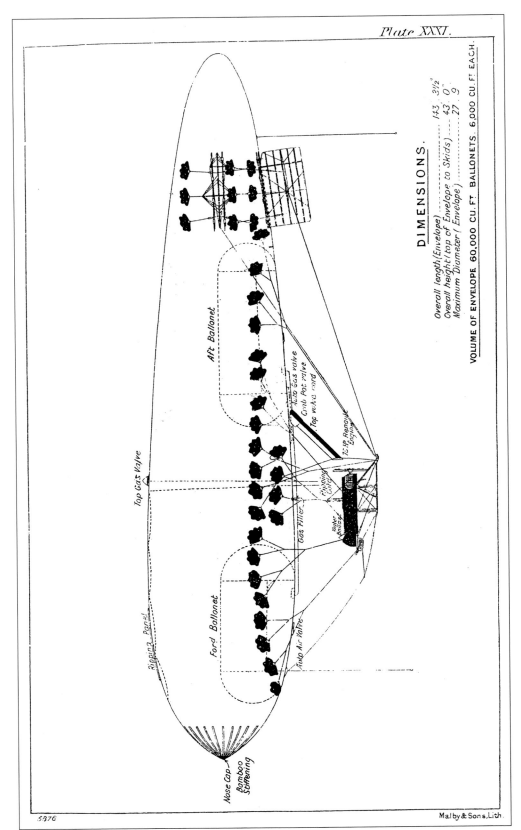

Nose Cap
Bamboo Stiffening

Ripping Panel

Top Gas Valve

Ford Ballonet

Aft Ballonet

Auto Gas valve
Crab Pot valve
Top valve cord

Gas Filler

Ripping Cord

Water Ballast

Auto Air Valve

75 H.P. Renault Engine.

DIMENSIONS.

Overall length (Envelope) ———————— 143′ 3½″
Overall height (top of Envelope to Skids) ——— 43′ 0″
Maximum Diameter (Envelope) ————— 27′ 9″

VOLUME OF ENVELOPE 60,000 CU. FT. BALLONETS 6,000 CU. FT. EACH.

5876

Malby & Sons, Lith.

General arrangement of SS airship, 'MF' type.

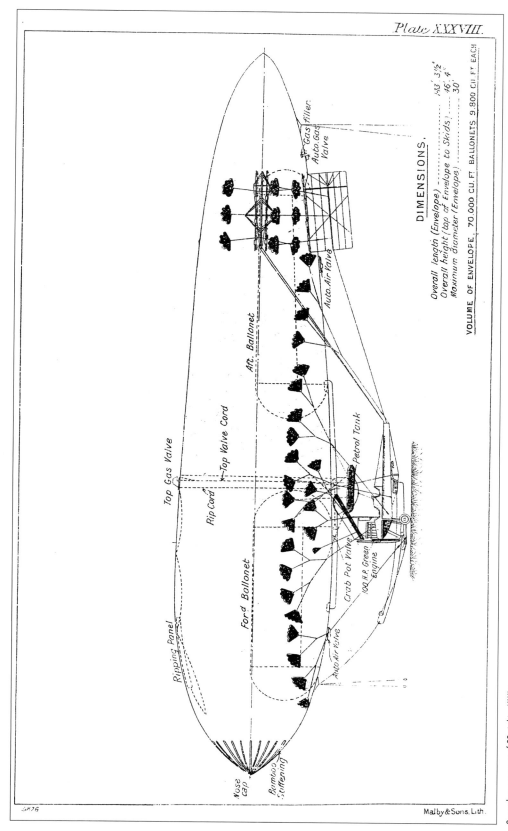

Plate XXXVIII.

Gas Filler.

Auto. Gas Valve.

Auto. Air Valve.

Aft. Ballonet.

Top Gas Valve.

Top Valve Cord

Rip Cord.

Ripping Panel.

For'd Ballonet.

Nose Cap.

Bamboo Stiffening.

Auto Air Valve.

Crab Pot Valve.

100 H.P. Green Engine.

Petrol Tank.

DIMENSIONS.

Overall length (Envelope) - - - - - - - - - - 143' 3½"
Overall height (top of Envelope to Skids.) - - - 46' 4"
Maximum diameter (Envelope.) - - - - - - - - 30'

VOLUME OF ENVELOPE, 70,000 CU. FT. BALLONETS 9,800 CU. FT. EACH.

Malby & Sons, Lith.

General arrangement of SS airship, 'AW' type.

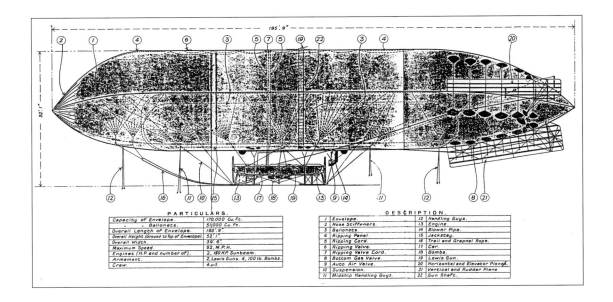

PARTICULARS.	
Capacity of Envelope.	170,000 Cu.Ft.
" " Ballonets.	51,000 Cu.Ft.
Overall Length of Envelope.	195'9".
Overall Height (Ground to Top of Envelope).	52'1".
Overall Width.	39'6".
Maximum Speed.	52, M.P.H.
Engines (H.P. and number of).	2, 150 H.P. Sunbeam.
Armament.	2, Lewis Guns. 4, 100 lb. Bombs.
Crew.	4 or 5.

DESCRIPTION.			
1	Envelope.	12	Handling Guys.
2	Nose Stiffeners.	13	Engine.
3	Ballonets.	14	Blower Pipe.
4	Ripping Panel.	15	Jackstay.
5	Ripping Cord.	16	Trail and Grapnel Rope.
6	Ripping Valve.	17	Car.
7	Ripping Valve Cord.	18	Bombs.
8	Bottom Gas Valve.	19	Lewis Gun.
9	Auto Air Valve.	20	Horizontal and Elevator Planes.
10	Suspension.	21	Vertical and Rudder Plane
11	Midship Handling Guys.	22	Gun Shaft.

General arrangement of 'Coastal' airship.

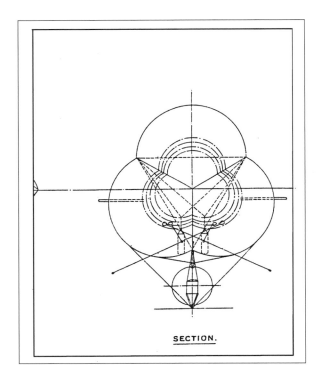

SECTION.

166

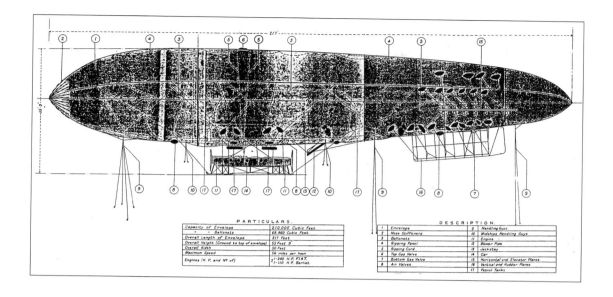

PARTICULARS.	
Capacity of Envelope	210,000 Cubic Feet.
" - Ballonets	68,860 Cubic Feet.
Overall Length of Envelope	217 Feet
Overall Height (Ground to top of envelope)	55 Feet 9"
Overall Width	50 Feet
Maximum Speed	56 miles per hour
Engines (H.P. and N° of)	2 1-240 H.P. FIAT. 1-110 H.P. Berlict.

DESCRIPTION.			
1	Envelope	9	Handling Guys
2	Nose Stiffeners	10	Midships Handling Guys
3	Ballonets	11	Engine
4	Ripping Panel.	12	Blower Pipe
5	Ripping Cord	13	Jackstay
6	Top Gas Valve	14	Car
7	Bottom Gas Valve	15	Horizontal and Elevator Planes
8	Air Valves	16	Vertical and Rudder Planes
		17	Petrol Tanks

General arrangement of 'C*' (Coastal Star) airship.

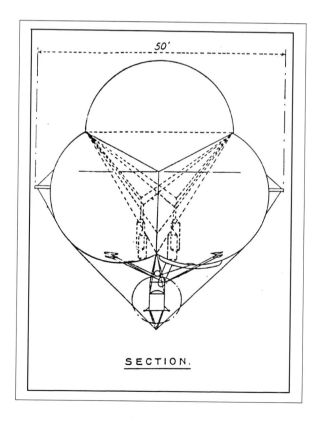

SECTION.

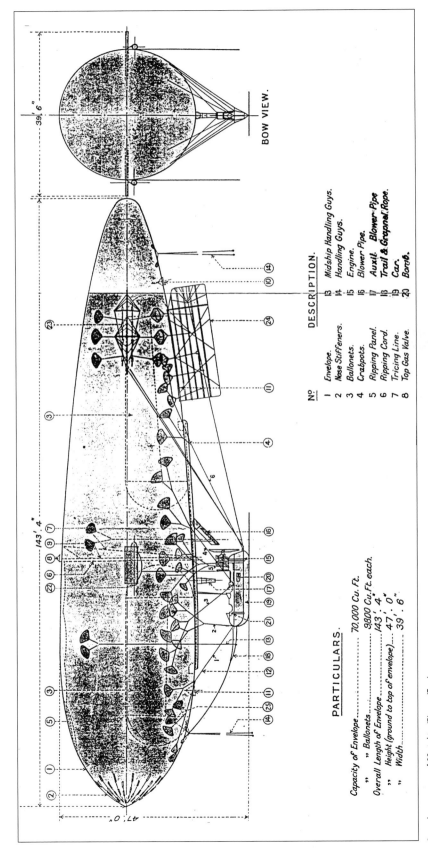

BOW VIEW.

DESCRIPTION.

№			
1	Envelope.	13	Midship Handling Guys.
2	Nose Stiffeners.	14	Handling Guys.
3	Ballonets.	15	Engine.
4	Crabpots.	16	Blower Pipe.
5	Ripping Panel.	17	Auxil. Blower-Pipe
6	Ripping Cord.	18	Trail & Grapnel Rope.
7	Tricing Line.	19	Car.
8	Top Gas Valve.	20	Bomb.

PARTICULARS.

Capacity of Envelope............ 70,000 Cu. Ft.
    ,,   ,, Ballonets............ 9800 Cu. Ft. each.
Overall Length of Envelope...... 143' 4".
    ,, Height (ground to top of envelope)... 47' 0".
    ,, Width .... 39' 6".

General arrangement of SS airship, 'Z' type (Zero).

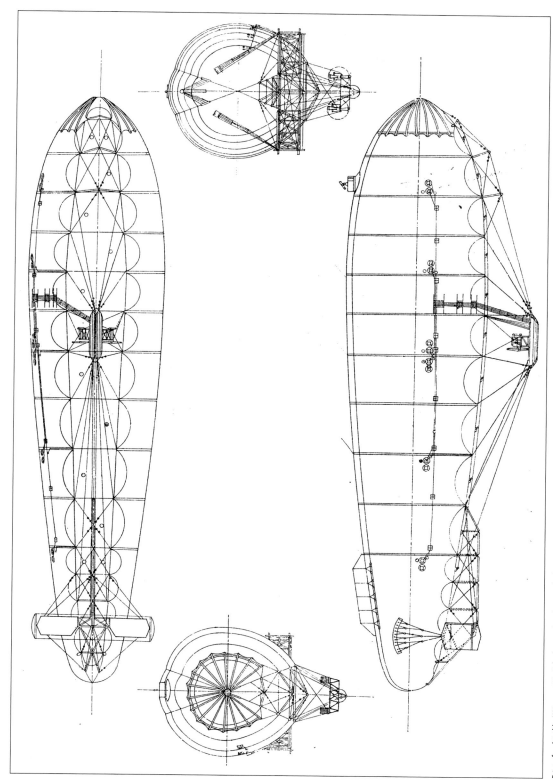

Print of a dirigible 'M' type. SR–1 had an enclosed car. A third engine was fitted on the roof.

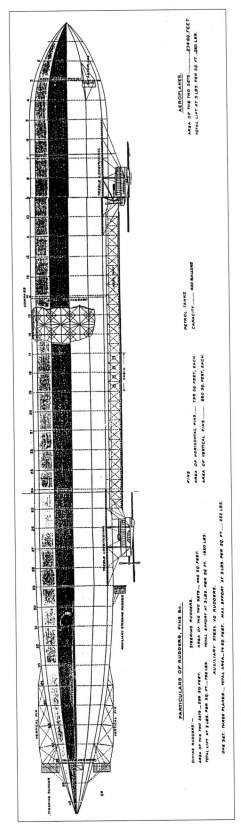

Naval Airship No. 1, as launched May 1911

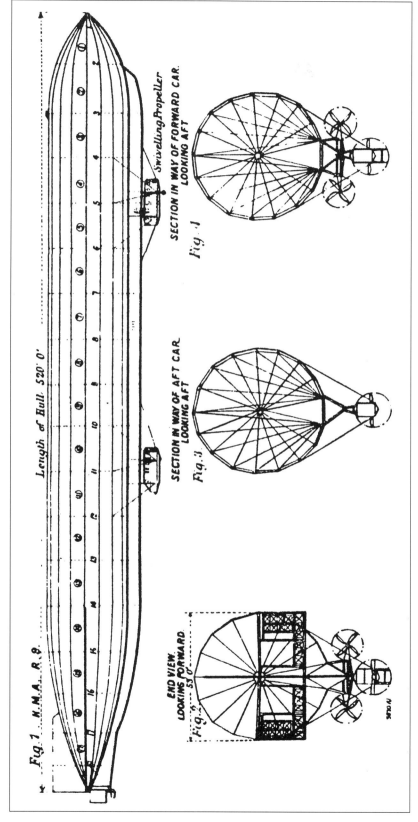

Drawing of HMA No. 9r.

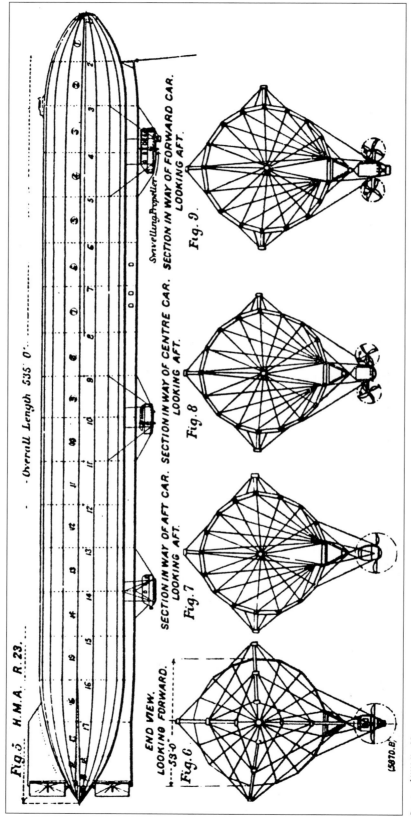

Fig. 5 H.M.A. R.23.

Overall Length 535' 0"

Swivelling Propeller

SECTION IN WAY OF AFT CAR. SECTION IN WAY OF CENTRE CAR. SECTION IN WAY OF FORWARD CAR.
LOOKING AFT. LOOKING AFT. LOOKING AFT.

END VIEW.
LOOKING FORWARD.
53'·0"

Fig. 6

Fig. 7

Fig. 8

Fig. 9

(5970.B.)

Drawing of HMA No. 23r.

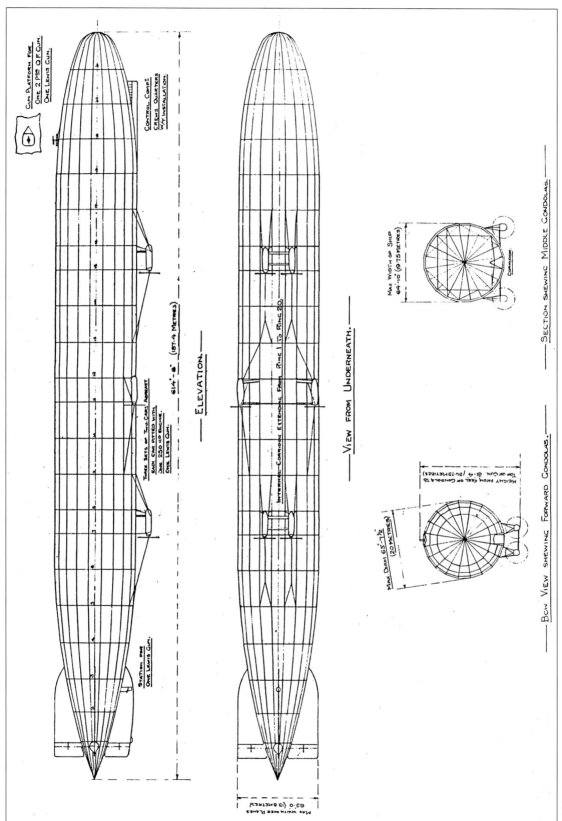

Rigid airships 31 and 32.

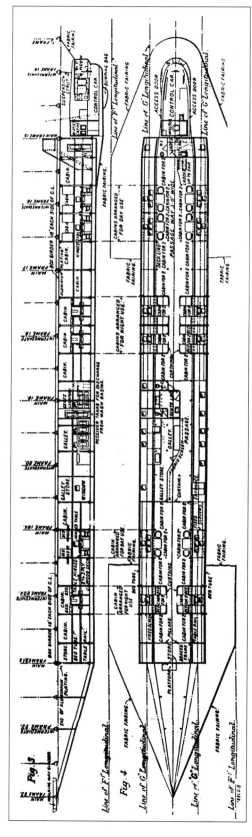

Passenger accommodation on airship R.36 (G-FAAF). Constructed by Messrs William Beardmore and Co., engineers, Inchinnan, near Glasgow.

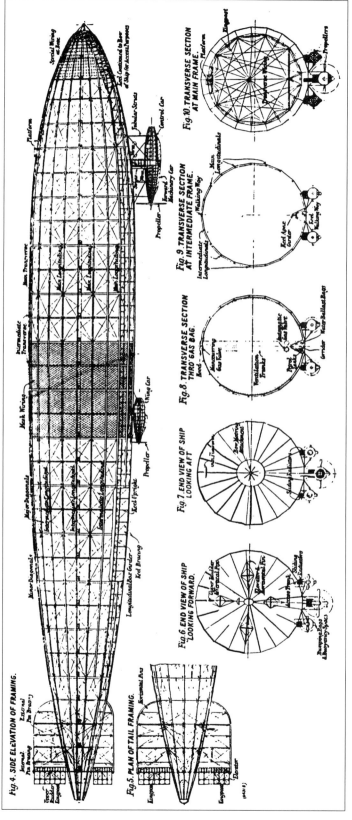

Fig. 4. SIDE ELEVATION OF FRAMING.

Fig. 5. PLAN OF TAIL FRAMING.

Fig. 6. END VIEW OF SHIP LOOKING FORWARD.

Fig. 7. END VIEW OF SHIP LOOKING AFT

Fig. 8. TRANSVERSE SECTION THRO' GAS BAG.

Fig. 9. TRANSVERSE SECTION AT INTERMEDIATE FRAME.

Fig. 10. TRANSVERSE SECTION AT MAIN FRAME.

Vickers-built R.80.

RNAS AIRSHIP STATIONS AND SHEDS

The natural element of airships is the air. Within it they can perform reasonably well. It is when airships are on the ground that the real trouble starts – especially in bad weather. Unlike an aeroplane which is heavier than air, airships in flying condition are extremely buoyant. This means that in the slightest wind, handling them on the ground is a very tricky business. Their huge bulk is a further complication: even the small non-rigids such as the 'SS' and 'SSZ' classes required up to a hundred men to man-handle them in a strong breeze! When the brand-new R.100 was taken out of her shed at Howden for her maiden flight on 16 December 1929 it was a calm morning – specially chosen – but it still required 400 troops from York to accomplish the task.

From the earliest days it was necessary to provide a shed for each airship. Only when safely inside could they be considered truly secure. After 1919, mooring masts became a reasonable alternative, but during the heyday of the British airship, each ship was housed inside a shed. Pioneers such as Stanley and Willows used the shed in which the airship had been built as a base. Farnborough and Wormwood Scrubs, the seat of service lighter-than-air craft, initially built their sheds on an ad-hoc basis, subject to requirement.

However, the supply of 'SS' class ships in early 1915 and the 'Coastals' six months later demanded a standardisation of sheds. Likewise, when the rigid programme got under way in 1917–18, the new craft had to be accommodated.

The RNAS inherited much know-how when it took airships over from the Army on 1 July 1914. This included experience in 'mooring out' at sites in suitable woods, quarries, etc. Also, with a view to mobile warfare, a portable shed had been developed; this consisted of steel framework covered by canvas. It was a similar 'portable shed' which initially housed the early 'SS' ships at Capel, etc. However, these were soon followed by what became known as the 'Coastal' shed.

The 'Coastal' shed was basically 320 ft long, 120 ft wide and 80 ft high, although the dimensions varied slightly. These were permanent buildings usually clad in heavy-gauge corrugated iron and fitted with sliding doors at each end. They accommodated two 'Coastals' side by side, plus two 'SS' ships. Some war stations had two of these sheds which housed all their non-rigid ships, 'SSs', 'Coastals' and 'Zeros', etc.

It was the coming of the large rigid classes that caused major problems. The Admiralty deemed that, as with the 'Coastals', rigids would be housed side by side in double sheds. The sheds were huge: for example, the No. 1 rigid airship shed at Howden, built in 1916, was 703 ft long, 150 ft wide and 100 ft high. This was to house two '23' class ships. Larger sheds were required for the later '33' class, and the largest of all, the No. 2 shed at Howden, was a double shed, 750 ft × 300 ft × 130 ft. The construction of these huge sheds was one of the snags in airship operations. For example, the first Cardington

Portable SS-sheds being erected at Capel, 12 October 1915. (JMB/GSL Collection)

RNAS Luce Bay, 1918. The photograph shows hutted accommodation (right), the station HQ and administration block (bottom), and the 'Coastal' shed (with wind shields) (top centre). Note the gas plant and holder next to the shed. (Fleet Air Arm Museum)

shed (No. 1) was in its original form the biggest to be erected in Britain at that time, September–December 1916. Internal dimensions of 700 ft × 180 ft × 110 ft meant an awful lot of steel was required: this at a time when the country's war effort demanded steel for weapons, and was allocated on a priority basis.

The sheer physical task of building these sheds came under a little-known military corps, the Air Construction Corps. This naval outfit had been formed to build war stations for the RNAS. In preparation for the rigid airship fleet, which was constructed in purpose-built double sheds at Barrow (Vickers), Inchinnan (Beardmore), Barlow (Armstrong) and Cardington (Shorts), it was desirable to have rigid airship war stations down the East Coast, namely at Longside, East Fortune, Howden, Pulham and Kingsnorth. These looked after the North Sea patrols. Later a rigid shed was nearly completed at Lough Neagh in Northern Ireland for the proposed 'Atlantic' patrols of the '33' class ships, which the Armistice rendered unnecessary; and a rigid shed was also built at Cranwell in 1918, a base for training airship crews.

Initially, single sheds capable of housing two '23' class ships were built. Then, because of the increased size of the '33' class ships, only one could be fitted into these original buildings. Hence the next phase sheds were much larger, such as Pulham No. 2 and Howden No. 2.

Such was the vulnerability of rigid airships that they had to be housed for safety during bad weather. Therefore they had always to be within range of a 'secure' base. Figures have appeared stating that steel, which would have built a dozen naval destroyers, was used in rigid airship sheds alone, and at a time when Britain desperately needed destroyers! British rigid airships scarcely contributed to victory

The double shed at Howden, 1921. R.38 is inside. To give some idea of scale, the 'small' door in the centre was large enough to allow a normal railway engine and trucks to pass into the shed between the splayed feet of the centre partition. Railway tracks led from Howden Junction. (Ces Mowthorpe Collection)

in 1918. However, had the war carried on another two years, it may have been a different story. Finally, in the mid-1920s, when the Rigid Airship Programme took shape and the 5,000,000 cu ft R.100 and R.101 were conceived, the Cardington shed was enlarged. The 'new' No. 2 shed at Pulham was dismantled, enlarged, and re-erected alongside its sister at Cardington, where they can be seen today.

The only other shed which could accommodate the two huge rigids was Howden's No. 2 double shed. R.100 was built there by Vickers' subsidiary, the Airship Guarantee Co Ltd. This shed was dismantled and sold as scrap after being deemed unsafe in the 1930s.

All airship sheds were built into the 'prevailing' winds and had doors at either end. Even this caused problems with airships being slammed against the doorway if caught

by a gust when half-way out. A further refinement was screens, which were as long as the shed and extended out into the field. These protected the vulnerable airship as it was 'walked' out of its shed. Initially walked-out by a large ground crew, after the war manpower was partially replaced at some stations by a tractor. Pulham converted a tank, fitting a small lattice mast to its upper works. Even so, a ground crew was still needed to guide the rigid airships.

The gas used to lift the airships was hydrogen. This has to be produced in large quantities to supply a fleet of airships. Produced commercially, hydrogen was initially bought in and stored in bottles during the early pre-war days. The first airship stations were supplied with portable Silicol gas-plants capable of yielding 2,500 cu ft of hydrogen per hour. These were soon replaced by permanent Silicol gas-plants

P.6 landing in gusty conditions at Pulham, 1917. The ship is being piloted by Lt Cdr Cooke. Note the caterpillar tractor preparing to tow the ship into the shed. (JMB/GSL Collection)

yielding 10,000 cu ft per hour. A later hydrogen-producing plant using the water/steam/iron principle was available for large stations and these produced 14,000 cu ft per hour. Deep wells had to be sunk nearby, for supplying the water, while several medium-sized gasometers stored the hydrogen. Gas bottles were filled under pressure and used on mooring-out sites.

Due to the explosive quality of hydrogen when mixed with air, great care was required when producing this gas: the Silicol plants were specially sensitive. It is a tribute to all that there is only one recorded accident. At midday on 14 April 1917, the Silicol plant at Pulham exploded and two men were blown through the side of the gas-house. A Lt Wildmass and a rating were killed. Lt Mitten (the gas officer) and a civilian workman were covered in caustic soda and badly burned; Lts Bevington and Pollett and several others were also injured.

The RNAS and, later, Messrs Vickers extensively researched mooring airships to masts. The final version as used at Cardington and Montreal for the R.100 and R.101 programme was very sophisticated and completely successful. The American airship fleet which operated from 1926 into the 1960s made extensive use of masts and mechanical handling devices which owed much to Messrs Vickers and Capt Scott (lost in the R.101 disaster). The Germans, however, had discarded the use of masts for their airships before 1914.

The team at Farnborough designed a portable mooring mast and adapted several non-rigids by fitting a flexible joint into the nose cones. This method was used later by the RNAS at Dunkirk for mooring the Astra-Torres No. 3. In May 1911, No. 1r 'Mayfly' was successfully moored to a low mast in Cavendish Dock and weathered 45 m.p.h. gusts.

During 1918, mooring experiments really got under way at Pulham. All classes, non-rigid and rigid, were moored to various masts. Naturally, as the size of the ship increased, stronger masts and, equally important, stronger and more sophisticated mooring attachments to the ships themselves, were required. Pulham built two lattice-type masts for rigids, first the 'low' mast, and, as experience was gained, the 'high' mast. By 1920, non-rigids were relegated to 'sheds only' and work concentrated upon the large rigids: in July 1921, R.33 was moored to a temporary wooden mast at Croydon Airport while assisting police in traffic control.

Meanwhile, Vickers at Barrow-in-Furness had independently carried out an experimental programme for mooring airships. Although small non-rigids were used, and a satisfactory mooring mast designed and used experimentally, this programme was only part of the development of a proposed mast for rigids. Finally, as part of the R.100 and R.101 programme, the two teams pooled information which culminated in the building of the masts at Cardington and Montreal, both of which were used, though Montreal only once. (A third mast was built at Ismailia in Egypt.)

Although mooring to a mast used only a fraction of the manpower, and with experience could be accomplished in bad weather quite safely, it nevertheless required considerable practice on the part of both the airship captain and the tower officer. Pulham developed it to a fine art. Regrettably, the loss of R.101 and the consequent end of the British airship programme prevented this remarkable British invention fulfilling its potential.

RNAS HOWDEN: A TYPICAL WAR-STATION

Too far from the coast to successfully operate the original 'SS' class non-rigids, Howden was not commissioned until 15 March 1916. The first 'Coastal' did not arrive until 26 June 1916. Staffed with approximately 1,000 officers and ratings, plus civilian employees, control (in 1918) was still in Royal Naval hands, but the newly formed Royal Air Force took charge of the personnel after 1 April.

When hostilities ceased in 1918, Howden was the permanent base of two rigid airships, one 'North Sea' type, five 'Coastals' and six 'SSZs.' Two mooring out stations, Lowthorpe and Kirkleatham, came under its direct control. Complete facilities for the operation of lighter-than-air craft in wartime were incorporated, together with full maintenance equipment.

Situated to the north of Howden village, the site comprised approximately 1,000 acres. It was served by a branch line from the North Howden railway junction, which crossed the Bubwith road near the Spaldington fork and led directly over the airfield, with branch lines into No. 1 shed, No. 2 shed (1919), the coal store and gas plant. A weighbridge was incorporated close to the latter. An airfield road cut across at right angles from the Bubwith road for several hundred yards until petering out past the sheds. This road was crossed by the railway line which had a lifting gantry immediately north of this intersection.

All the airship sheds had large windshields extending outboard from the shed doors. At Howden the railway line passed through No.

1 shed's windshield and a gate was closed across the line if the shed doors were opened. This gate-post was only removed in the early 1970s!

'Coastal' C.11 was the first airship to arrive, flying from Kingsnorth on 26 June 1916. To house the proposed 'Coastals', two sheds were erected initially, 'Coastal' shed 'A', 323 ft × 120 ft 5 in × 81 ft, and 'Coastal' shed 'B', 320 ft × 110 ft × 80 ft. Each could comfortably house two 'Coastals' with at least one complete 'SSZ'. During December 1916 a large rigid shed, No. 1, 703 ft × 148 ft 11 in × 100 ft 8 in, was completed to accommodate the proposed '23' class rigid which it was hoped would be flying by that time. 1918 saw No. 2 rigid shed laid down. Some 750 ft long, 300 ft wide and 130 ft high, it was not completed until 1919. Its purpose was to house two of the new '33' class ships.

The flying area, including the sheds and service units, was on the southern side of the above-mentioned airfield road, together with the gate-house, guardroom, NAAFI and coal store. North of this roadway were the jail, motor unit, met office, W/T hut and masts, and station HQ. In 1918, WAAF quarters were built between the W/T masts. Beyond the station HQ was the parade ground, with the barrack huts behind. A number of NCO huts brought the accommodation units up to the railway line.

Further back was the officers mess, water tower and wells. In front of the wells was the water gas plant (hydrogen), which was backed by four gas-holders totalling 2,000,000 cu ft. The power house was between the gas plant and the road. Stores were next and, finally, well out in the field, was the ammunition dump. Behind the stores was the early Silicol gas plant which was superseded by the larger water gas plant in May 1917.

Within several days C.11 was joined by C.4, and the first operational flights of both took place on 3 July 1916. C.19 arrived on strength on 11 September, followed by C.21 on 26 September 1916. Next, Parseval P.4 transferred from Barrow-in-Furness, making her first flight from her new base on 27 December 1916. She was slightly damaged through a heavy landing but repaired by the New Year when she was used for training No. 9 Rigid Trials Flight under Cdr Masterman.

Between 26 June and 31 December 1916, a total of 521 flying hours was completed by the Howden airships. Howden's complement at the end of the year was 25 officers and 476 men, including 139 men of the Air Service Construction Corps. During 1917, the number of airships was greatly increased. Rigids No. 9 and No. 25 arrived, together with two Vickers-built Parsevals, Nos. 5 and 7. Sistership No. 6 operated for part of 1917 from Howden but left for Cranwell on 6 August.

Meanwhile, on 21/22 July, No. 9 made a British record flight (up to that date) of 26 hours, 35 minutes, covering 430 miles. Regrettably she was seriously damaged while entering her shed on 29 October and hence out of commission for the rest of the year. 'Coastals' C.4, C.10 and C.21 were all flying from Howden while C.11 was being repaired after crashing at Scarborough. Repaired as C.11A, she was lost in the Humber during her trial flight on 19 July 1917. SS.9A was on charge in November after surviving a forced landing.

The end of 1917 saw Howden with a complement of 40 officers and 612 ratings. A total of 2,086 flying hours had been achieved, the best months being April, June and July with 150, 226 and 258 hours respectively. The mooring out ground established at Gosforth Park, Newcastle, was closed on 1 October when soldiers used for landing the airships left the district.

The greatest amount of patrol and escort work was carried out by the 'Coastals' and exceeded all expectations. The old P.4 moved down to Pulham during March, and P.6 transferred permanently to Cranwell for training purposes on 6 August. P.5 was flown on trials on 12 November. P.7's first trial flight was 22 December 1917. The first months of 1918 saw the new non-rigid 'SSZ' class ships start to arrive at Howden, SSZ.32, SSZ.58 and SSZ.38 all becoming operational during March and early April. It was during the latter month that the mooring out site at Lowthorpe Woods began operations. SSZ.23, which had been sold to the US Navy, operated from there in May 1918 together with SSZ.32 and SSZ.38. SSZ.32 was wrecked (without casualties) near Lowthorpe on 19 May and replaced by SSZ.63 six days later. No. 25 had been plagued with 'surging' of her gas-bags and was relegated to Cranwell for training duties, with her successor R.26 'on station' in May.

Several of the old 'Coastals' were replaced by the improved 'C*' class. C*4 and C*2 both arrived early in 1918, together with 'Zeros' SSZ.54 and SSZ.55. No. 9 left Howden after repairs had been carried out following her accident on 29 October 1917, and a 'North Sea' class non-rigid replaced her. Several other 'NS' class ships were hangared at Howden during this period while en route to East Fortune and other northerly war stations.

A further mooring out station at Kirkleatham, near Redcar, was commissioned during May and served by the above-mentioned 'Zeros', with the addition of SSZ.62.

June saw the arrival at Howden of Britain's newest rigid and the first of the modified '23' class, known as the '23x' class. Commissioned on the 29th, she was an improvement over her predecessors No. 9 and R.26.

Between her launching and sudden demise on 16 August, R.27 flew 89 hours 40 minutes. Her ending was interesting. SSZ.23 had been packed for transport to America by her US naval crew. In the process she had been given a new envelope. The American crew then rigged the old envelope to a 'spare' car, intending to present the RNAS with a 'new' unnumbered 'Zero'! This work was being done in No. 1 rigid shed, which at that time contained R.27, SSZ.38, SSZ.54 and the packed-up SSZ.23. The hybrid 'Zero' had been rigged complete when the W/T operator checked the wireless set. A spark from this ignited petrol in the 'car' and the resultant inferno destroyed all the ships! A rating who was on look-out in the shed roof lost his life in the disaster. (The shed remained usable although the heat had distorted the corrugated iron roof which began to leak badly during inclement weather.)

Mid-1918 saw the arrival at Howden of the first Women's Auxiliary Air Force personnel who were housed in their own block on the western side of the station HQ. Work was also started on No. 2 rigid shed which was eventually meant to house two of the new '33' class rigids under construction. Owing to the run-down of forces after the Armistice, this hangar was not completed until 1919.

With the formation of the Royal Air Force on 1 April 1918, Howden, like all RNAS airship establishments, became part RAF, part RN. The personnel all belonged to the RAF but the airships and their equipment were still on charge to the Royal Navy! This state of affairs continued until Howden finally closed down in September 1921.

The three months prior to the Armistice saw a steady expansion of work at Howden but the most important event was the unscheduled arrival of the new R.31 on 6 November. Having left Cardington for her war station of East Fortune under the command of Cdr Sparling, R.31 suffered a number of breakages to her frames and girders (she was a wooden airship based on Schutte-Lanz principles) and consequently landed for repairs at Howden. She was hangared in No. 1 rigid shed which had been damaged in the R.27 fiasco.

The cessation of hostilities and the immediate run-down of the armed forces saw the wooden airship gradually deteriorate beneath the leaking shed. Eventually all salvageable material was removed and the R.31's wooden framework sold for firewood in July 1919 (the dealer found out too late that all the wood had been 'treated' and 'fireproofed'!). Her total flying-time was just 8 hours 55 minutes.

Newer classes of airships soon began to replace the originals. The last 'Coastals', C.5 and C.9, were replaced by 'Coastal Star' class ships, C*6, C*7, C*9 and C*10 all being on strength at Howden during the latter end of 1918 and early 1919. 'Zeros' flown from here and the mooring out stations were SSZ.31, SSZ.33, SSZ.56 and SSZ.64. Three of the 'North Sea' class, NS–8, NS–9 and NS–16, are known to have operated out of Howden during 1919.

The airship programme suffered from cancellations after November 1918. Because Howden was a major airship station and had a new shed capable of housing rigids R.33 and R.34, it escaped closure. Although considerably run down from its wartime complement, it still remained, together with Pulham and East Fortune, a very important station so long as Britain continued to operate lighter-than-air craft.

Apart from its prominence with regard to the new rigids, much work had to be done over the North Sea clearing away the minefields laid by both sides during the war. For this duty the airship was ideal. During the year, the 'Zeros' were gradually replaced by the newer 'SS-Twins' and at various times SST–3, SST–4, SST–5, SST–7, SST–9, SST–10, SST–11 and SST–12 were on strength.

During 1919, airships, which were proving expensive, became the unwanted 'children' of both the RAF and RN because of the economic and political situation. This brought about extreme cut-backs in their operation and between August and September 1919 most of Britain's airship fleet was deleted. Only the most modern ships were retained and the building programme was firmly axed. Still, with her large double shed and strategic position, Howden again survived to remain in business, albeit on a drastically reduced scale.

After R.34's successful trans-Atlantic flight, she was overhauled at Howden. R.32 was also based there during 1920–21, and improved radio facilities were laid on. Experiments with mooring masts at Pulham had shown that these were essential for successful rigid operations and so preparations were made to build a similar mast at Howden (though for financial reasons this was never completed).

During her overhaul R34 was fitted with nose mooring gear. R.33, which had moored many hours at the Pulham mast, was often seen at Howden. 1920 saw virtually the end of the smaller non-rigids that still remained in service, with the exception of the 'North Sea' class. Howden operated NS–8, NS–9 and NS–16 with others 'in transit' until the class ended operations in 1921.

Finally, the rigid building programme came

to a halt in this country, with the exception of R.38 still under construction at Cardington. Everything hinged upon a successful sale of this airship. Britain would build airships for the rest of the world, as she had built battleships, and train their crews, therefore ensuring a healthy programme for herself.

The future of large airships in Britain appeared to be secured when the Americans decided to buy R.38 in 1920 and a crew was sent to Howden to train for the task of flying her back across the Atlantic. Although the Americans insisted upon being trained in a 'metal' rigid, R.33 was under repair and R.34 was still being overhauled so they commenced on the wooden R.32, prior to R.34 becoming operational about January 1921. The Howden Attachment USN began training on 21 April 1920 by stripping and overhauling R.32. First flights began on 11 August and continued until March 1921 when they transferred to R.80 after the loss of R.34.

R.34 took off in January 1920, fresh from overhaul, on a trials/navigation exercise over the North Sea. In deteriorating weather she struck the North Yorkshire Moors near Guisborough but managed to return to Howden the next day. Unfortunately, after safely reaching her base she was unable to get into her shed owing to a rising wind. Moored outside on the field, the gale beat her into the ground and next morning she was found to be so badly damaged that she was broken up on the spot.

This left the US crew with only the wooden R.32 which was due to be taken out of service in May 1921. Therefore, in March, R.80 was placed at their disposal and consequently R.32 was broken up in No. 1 shed during the course of pressure tests in conjunction with the National Physical Laboratory. During this period, Howden operated 'North Seas', with two always being 'on station'.

Finally, R.38 was completed at Cardington and her third flight, on 17–18 July 1921, was up at Howden. Unfortunately, damage was sustained to several girders and repairs had to be carried out before the next flight, which took place on 23 August. Returning to Howden the next day, after remaining out all night, R.38 broke up over Hull during high-speed turning trials. Falling into the Humber in two pieces, one section on fire, there were only five survivors, one her captain. Most of the Americans were aboard and lost their lives.

The loss of R.38 struck the final blow to British airships. All work was brought to a standstill and finally the airship station at Howden closed down. The last flight took place on 20 September 1921 when R.80 left for Pulham with the CO on board. Thus ended the first era of one of Britain's largest and most important operational airship stations.

From September 1921 the fixtures at Howden slowly deteriorated. Wooden huts rotted, drains filled up and the remains of the station slowly became overrun with grass and foliage. The one feature that remained apparently untouched was the huge No. 2 shed. Completed in 1919, its 750 ft × 300 ft steel structure, covered in heavy-gauge corrugated iron, dominated the skyline for miles around.

Howden was given a new lease of life early in 1924, when the newly formed Airship Guarantee Co, a subsidiary of Vickers, was awarded a contract to build a 5,000,000 cu ft rigid passenger-carrying airship. The company leased Howden from the Air Ministry, which allowed the company to re-condition the 'new' No. 2 shed, erect buildings and use the airfield for the construction and flight trials of the later-named R.100.

During 1925, a working-party from Vickers arrived to re-mould Howden into something like an 'airship constructor's yard'. The huge 7.75-acre floor of No. 2 shed was littered with debris. At one end was a vixen's lair, complete with the remains of hundreds of hens! But, gradually, order was restored and the brick annexes to one side made into useful stores and offices. The water and sewage plants became operational and a hydrogen generating plant installed adjacent to the north wall of the shed. Thus at the end of 1926 most of the old heaps of rubble and broken-down buildings had been removed and in their place were nearly twenty bungalows, occupied by the staff and their families.

Because the shed was old and in an exposed position, much anxiety was caused whenever a storm blew up. In bad weather a standing watch of riggers stood by for the first signs of trouble. Inside the shed, R.100 slowly took shape. The huge transverse frames were first constructed on the floor, then hoisted to the roof and hung centrally. The next frame was built and hung the same, then the two were joined together by the longitudinal girders. In this way the ship slowly reached completion.

Although ready for her trials in November 1929, R.100 was not brought out of her shed until 16 December 1929 for a variety of reasons. That morning, however, saw the beautiful lines of R.100 emerge from her birthplace at approximately 07.30 hours. Without any mechanical handling aids, it had been necessary to 'import' several hundred troops from York to assist in this delicate manoeuvre. After ballasting up, R.100 gently lifted, circled Howden several times, and left – never to return.

For the second time in its brief life Howden slowly ground to a halt. Until the R.100 proved herself superior to her government-built sistership, R.101, no more rigids would be built. Gradually, however, with R.100's successful trans-Atlantic crossing behind them, the Airship Guarantee Co cautiously prepared to build her successors. Tragically, R.101 crashed at Beauvais, in France, in the early hours of 5 October 1930. This brought airship matters to a head. The government decided to finally suspend all airship activities and to break R.100 up in her shed at Cardington. Consequently the design team at Howden were dispersed and sacked in December 1930. Howden's huge No. 2 shed was finally dismantled and sold for scrap in the mid-1930s.

In the 1990s the only remains of the airship station are a few foundations scattered around. A golf course with its clubhouse occupy the southern side of the old airfield.

BIBLIOGRAPHY AND SOURCES

PRIMARY SOURCES

AIR 1.2307	215/19
AIR 1.2308	215/20
AIR 1.2309	215/21
AIR 1.2314	222/1
AIR 1.2315	222/6/A
AIR 1.2397	267/1, 267/9
AIR 1.2398	267/27
AIR 1.2421	305/18/4
AIR 1.2654	6/324
AIR 1.2682	204/282/2
AIR 2.6/1	197/RU.8894, 8895, 9331, 9320, 8892, (174–190) M.R. (5241–55253)(1592–1599).

AIR 2. Codes 30–45 (1897–1920)

PUBLISHED SECONDARY SOURCES

Airship Department Admiralty: all classes of Airship Handbooks.

Airship Department Admiralty: State of development of Airship Service.

Abbot, P., *Airship: The story of R.34*. Adams & Dart, Bath, 1975.

Abbot, P., *The British Airship at War, 1914–1918*. Terence Dalton, Lavenham, 1989.

Chamberlain, C., *Airships Cardington*. Terence Dalton, Lavenham, 1984.

Connon, P., *Aeronautical History of the Cumbria, Dumfries & Galloway Region*. St. Patricks Press, Penrith, 1984.

Gamble, C.F.S., *The Story of a North Sea Air Station*.

Higham, R., *The British Rigid Airship. 1908–1931*. G.T. Foulis, London, 1961.

HMSO, Various Admiralty *Monthly Orders*.

Jackson, *Airships*.

Kinsey, G., *Pulham Pigs*.

McKinty, A., *The Father of British Airships*. (E.T. Willows biography.) William Kimber & Co. Ltd, London, 1972.

Masefield, P., *To Ride the Storm*. William Kimber & Co. Ltd, London, 1982.

Meager, G., *My Airship Flights*. William Kimber & Co. Ltd, London, 1970.

Raleigh, W. and Jones, A., *The War in the Air*.

Robinson, D., *Giants in the Sky*. G.T. Foulis, London, 1973.

Reminiscences. The story of RNAS Polegate.

Sinclair, Capt J.A., *Famous Airships of the World*. Fred Muller Ltd, London, 1959.

Toland, J., *Giants in the Sky*. Fred Muller Ltd, London, 1957.
Turpin, Brian, *The Coastal Airship*. Cross & Cockade.
Turpin, Brian, *The Sea Scouts*. Cross & Cockade.
Ventry & Kolesnil, *Airship Saga*. Blandford Press, Poole, 1982.
Williams, T.B., *Airship Pilot No. 28*. William Kimber and Co. Ltd, London, 1974.

INDEX